Aristotle
at Afternoon Tea

Aristotle at Afternoon Tea

the rare Oscar Wilde

Edited and Introduced by
John Wyse Jackson

FOURTH ESTATE · *London*

First published in Great Britain in 1991 by
Fourth Estate Limited
289 Westbourne Grove
London W11 2QA

A catalogue record for this book is available from the British Library

ISBN 1-85702-015-4

Phototypeset by Intype, London
Printed in Great Britain by Biddles Ltd, Guildford

*This book is dedicated
to the memory of my father,
Robert Wyse Jackson*

Contents

Introduction

Only the skeptics (or idlers or aesthetes) escape, because they *propose* nothing, because they – humanity's true benefactors – undermine fanaticism's purposes, analyze its frenzy.

E. M. Cioran: *A Short History of Decay*

Oscar Wilde needs no introduction. His plays remain firmly in print, and they are frequently revived on stage. His novel, *The Picture of Dorian Gray*, is available in several editions, and is still widely read. His fairy tales are children's classics, and every Christmas, it seems, brings another collection of his epigrams and witty sayings. Two volumes of his letters are in paperback. Most of the above, as well as Wilde's poems, can be found in large tomes with titles like *The Complete Oscar Wilde*, to be had, as they say, in 'all good bookshops'. Biographies of Wilde have achieved high sales in recent years, and his life, whose pattern echoed the celebrated expedition of the Grand Old Duke of York, is still a subject of controversy, speculation, and television documentaries.

What, then, is this book?

It does not pretend to be scholarly. There are no notes or critical apparatus. What is contained in these pages is purely a selection of the writings that Wilde produced in order to allow him to earn enough money to live up to his own standards. These essays, reviews and lectures, which contain some of his most important, most interesting, or simply most entertaining work, have been unavailable to the general reader for years. Although there was an academic collection in the 1960s which overlapped with this, nothing here is currently in print. This book stems immediately from a wish to share the pleasure I felt when I happened across that great and courageous memorial to Oscar edited by his friend Robbie Ross: *The Complete Works of Oscar Wilde* (1908). From this many-volumed work the texts here are unashamedly taken.

At the end of the 1870s, Oscar Wilde found himself in the unpleasant position of having to earn his living. Furnished with his Bachelor of Arts degree, he had left Oxford, there having paid almost as much attention to his style of dress as he did to his studies. London life was congenial to him, and he rapidly became a man about town, attending first nights, writing much poetry and two unsatisfactory plays, and cultivating a large number of influential friends and acquaintances. He began to make his name. The magazine *Punch* caricatured him as the first among aesthetes, and Gilbert and Sullivan guyed him in their light opera, *Patience*.

It was *Patience*, which was running successfully in New York, that gave Wilde the opportunity to extend his reputation and to earn some money. As the model for Gilbert and Sullivan's 'Bunthorne' in the opera, he was already a celebrity in the New World, and he embarked upon a lecture tour, explaining to the good folk of America the philosophy of the aesthetic movement, and enjoying a great deal of publicity while he did so. By the end of 1884 he had also lectured widely in Britain and Ireland. Four of Wilde's lectures are included in this book.

By 1885, Wilde had begun writing professionally. His work appeared regularly in the *Dramatic Review* and the *Pall Mall Gazette*, and he contributed articles to several other magazines and papers. In 1887 he became editor of *The Woman's World*, where he was to remain for two not very hard-working years. Here, he produced a fairly regular column of literary notes, which consisted chiefly of batch reviews of almost uniformly forgettable novels or slim volumes of poems. Miss Edith Oenone Somerville (later to be co-author of the *Irish R.M.* stories) in a letter (written to Violet Martin in 1888) describes attempting to sell articles to the genial editor:

. . . I went down to Oscar yesterday . . . He is a great fat oily beast. He pretended the most enormous interest . . . but it was all of no

avail . . . He languidly took the sonnets and is to return them by post.
He talked great rot that 'French subjects should be drawn by French artists'
– I was near telling him, as Dr Johnson said – 'who drives fat oxen
must himself be fat'. He assumed deep interest in the 'Miss Martins',
asked if they were all married: I said 'mostly all'. He was kind enough
to say that Edith (Martin) was so pretty and nice – and bulged his long
fat red cheeks into an affectionate grin at the thought of her. He then
showed me a book of very indifferent French sketches – was foully civil,
and so goodbye.

Edith Somerville was naturally peeved that Wilde would not
accept any of her prose pieces for *The Woman's World*, but then,
Edith Somerville *was* naturally peeved. Besides, Oscar in the
flesh could be rather overwhelming. What shines through almost
all his work, however, and it is easily overlooked, is his gentleness. He did not hurt people gratuitously, or even when they
might have deserved it. His old mentor from Trinity College,
Dublin, John Pentland Mahaffy, *ought* to have been amused by
'Aristotle at Afternoon Tea', the review of his book which gives
this collection its title. One suspects, however, that he was not.
In his reviews of even the worst books (a few of which are
represented here) Wilde is light in tone; his wit is no bludgeon.
True, he points out infelicities, but in order to make the reader
laugh, and not to make the writer cry.

Of course, Wilde did not spend all his time reviewing bad
books. He spots the young poet Yeats, and writes perceptively
on Dostoevsky, Balzac, Ben Jonson, and his beloved Keats. His
friend Lily Langtry gets a puff, and Whistler is teased and
admired in the same breath. Idiosyncratic discussions on the
relationships between art and dress, and between dress and
women, give way to a useful survey of women poets. There are
articles of social observation, and observations on social art.

Throughout, Wilde is developing, refining and practising his
own particular philosophy. 'L'Envoi', an introduction to his
friend Rennell Rodd's book of lyrics, *Rose Leaf and Apple Leaf*,
was written in 1882 on the way back from his triumphant lecture
tour in America. Although it is laid on with a very thick brush,
it is the earliest clear exposition of the thoughts and feelings
behind Wilde's brand of aestheticism.

One of the great delights in anything written by Oscar Wilde is its clarity and its fluency. Like his compatriot, Bernard Shaw, he wrote well because he always knew precisely what he wanted to say. With neither writer does one get a sense of the hard work that must go into good writing. But Wilde was invariably the more elegant.

Two factors colour the modern reader's appreciation of Wilde's achievement. There is a cloud that hangs over our reading of Wilde: our knowledge of what was to befall him. There is also regret that we shall never hear his conversation. I append two contrasting glimpses of Oscar Wilde, the man:

The following report (spelling and grammar as originally published) of his prison years is taken from *Bruno's Weekly* (22 January, 1916).

The Story of Oscar Wilde's Life and Experience in Reading Gaol

by his warder

I remember, before he was transferred from Wandsworth Prison, the governor of Reading Gaol said to us 'A certain prisoner is about to be transferred here, and you should be proud to think the Prison Commissioners have chosen Reading Gaol as the one most suitable for this man to serve the remainder of his sentence in.'

The governor never told us the name, but directly the prisoner arrived, we saw that C.3.3. which was his prison letter and number, afterwards made famous by him, thus signing the 'Ballad of Reading Gaol' was none other than Oscar Wilde.

The probable cause for his transfer from Wandsworth Prison was his inability to comply with the regulation tasks allotted to his class of prisoner. On one or two occasions he had been brought up before the governor for idleness at oakum-picking or talking.

I remember my first sight of the fallen literary idol of whom all the world was then talking in terms of infamy. A tall figure with a large head and fat, pendulous cheeks, with hair that curled artistically, and a hopeless look in his eyes – that was Oscar Wilde as I first met him.

Not even the hideous prison garb, or c.3.3. the badge of ignominy he bore could altogether hide the hair of distinction and ever-present intellectual force that lifted him always far above 'the herd of brutes', as he so bitterly afterwards styled his fellow convicts and himself. From the first it was apparent to us that he was totally unfit for manual work, or hardships of any kind, and he was treated accordingly.

He was no good for anything – except writing, and that as a rule, has small place inside a prison. But on account of his former greatness a small concession was made him, and he was allowed to read and write as much as he liked.

Had this boon not been granted him he would, I am confident, have pined away and died. He was so unlike other men. Just a bundle of brains – and that is all.

When he arrived his hair was long and curly, and it was ordered to be cut at once.

It fell to my lot as warder in charge to carry out this order, and never shall I forget it.

To Oscar Wilde it seemed as though the clipping of his locks, and thus placing him on the same level as the closely shorn, bullet-headed prisoners round him was the last drop in the cup of sorrow and degradation which he had to drain to the bitter dregs.

'Must it be cut,' he cried piteously to me. 'You don't know what it means to me,' and the tears rolled down his cheeks.

It must seem somewhat ludicrous to some who do not know as I do, what a curiously constituted characer was that of Oscar Wilde, but I know it cut me to the heart to have to be the person to cause him his crowning shame. Warders have feelings, though their duty will not always allow them to show it.

The only task Wilde was put to was to act as a 'schoolmaster's orderly', which was in the nature of a great privilege, for it meant that he could take charge of the books and go round with them to other prisoners, besides having the pick of the literature for himself. Strange as it may seem considering his literary bent, he failed to accomplish even this task satisfactorily.

Chiefly he remained in his cell occupied with his books, of which in his cell he had a large supply, consisting of poetical works and foreign authors. On his table was always a manuscript book – full of writing in some foreign language – French or Italian I believe, and Wilde often seemed busily engaged writing in this.

I think this must have been *De Profundis* – the work of self-analysis that has just been published.

His hair was always kept closely cut until about five months before his discharge and I remember when he was told it need not be prison-cropped any more owing to his impending release, how pleased he seemed. And he was a man who so seldom lifted his bowed head of shame to smile.

Wilde was superstitious to a degree, and I recall one striking incident that proved his superstitious fears to be well grounded.

I was sweeping the walls of his cell, for he seldom followed the prison regulations with regard to scrupulously cleaning his cell daily, and I disturbed a spider which darted across the floor.

As it made off I raised my foot and killed it, when I saw Wilde looking at me with eyes of horror.

'It brings bad luck to kill a spider,' he said. 'I shall hear worse news than any I have yet heard.'

At the time I paid little attention to it, but the following morning he received the news that his mother, whom he had deeply loved and honoured, had died, and that his shame had hastened her end.

The saddest story I know of Wilde was one day when his solicitor called to see him to get his signature, I think, to some papers in the divorce proceedings then being instituted by his wife – a suit which, of course, Wilde did not defend.

Unknown to Wilde his wife had accompanied the solicitor, but she did not wish her husband to see her.

The interview with the solicitor took place in the consultation room, and Wilde sat at a table with his head on his hands opposite the lawyer.

Outside, in the passage with me, waited a sad figure in deepest mourning. It was Mrs Wilde – in tears.

Whilst the consultation was proceeding in the 'solicitor's room', Mrs Wilde turned to me and begged a favour. 'Let me have one glimpse of my husband,' she said, and I could not refuse her.

So silently I stepped on one side, Mrs Wilde cast one long, lingering glance inside, and saw the convict-poet, who, in deep mental distress himself, was totally unconscious (that any eyes) save those of the stern lawyer and myself witnessed his degradation.

A second later, Mrs Wilde, apparently labouring under deep emotion, drew back and left the prison with the solicitor.

I fancy Wilde, when she saw him, was putting the final signature to the divorce papers, and I do not know if she ever saw her unhappy husband again. I do not think she ever did.

At exercise, when he tramped what he called 'The Fools' Parade' with his companions of 'The Devil's Brigade', he would pace along with bended head as though deep in thought and usually muttering snatches of prose or verse from his favourite authors.

He took a most sympathetic interest in the sorrows and troubles of other prisoners, and commented fiercely on what he called the brutality of the prison system when a warder was suspended and finally dismissed for putting biscuits in the cell of a young prisoner whom Wilde believed to have been crying from hunger . . .

Wilde told me that those moments when the bell rang out, and his imagination conjured up the execution scene, were the most awful in a time rich in horrors.

I always found Wilde extremely goodnatured, and he wrote several little things out for me.

I had recently been married, and a certain weekly paper offered a silver tea service to the young couple who could give the best reason why this service should be given to them.

I told Wilde of this, and he wrote out several witty 'reasons' which I have kept. Here are some, very apt, which should have secured the tea service.

1 Because evidently spoons are required, and my girl and I are two.
2 Because it would suit us to a T (tea).
3 Because we have good 'grounds' for wanting a coffee pot.
4 Because marriage is a game that should begin with a love set.
5 Because one cannot legally get married without a proper wedding service.

These are very witty, are they not? And he also wrote out a little essay suggesting the name of a baby boy that would be suitable for Diamond Jubilee Year.

Oscar Wilde wrote this out in his own hand, and gave it to me. It was written in ten minutes, and began:

Every baby born in the course of this great and historic year should have a name representative in some way of what this year signifies to the British Empire. That is clear. The only question is what is it to be?

St George would be a capital name – it is a real Christian name, and is borne by Mr St George Mivart, a well-known writer – the only objection to it is that it refers too specially to England, and leaves out St Patrick, St Andrew and St David.

Victor, the masculine equivalent to Victoria, would be good, but not the best possible . . .

People are sometimes christened Tertius and Decimus, as being the third and tenth sons. Why not call the boy Sexagesimus?

Thus the sixtieth year of her Majesty's reign would be commemorated. Still that is an awkward name, and would not make the youthful owner popular at school.

Well, we call girls Ruby, Pearl and other names of precious jewels, and the Irish call their babies 'My jewel', and the French, 'Très bijoux'. Mr Walter Pater, whose prose we all admire for its noble qualities, called one of his characters 'Emerald'. Jacinth, which is a precious stone, is also a Christian name – the same as Hyacinth and Amethyst.

Garnet is a Christian name and the name of a jewel. Lord Wolseley was Sir Garnet Wolseley.

There is also a name 'Royal'. It is a very good name, but not sufficiently distinguishing.

Diamond must be made a popular name, so I hope, concluded Mr Wilde, to hear it has been given to our baby boy.

As a warder, I take my hat off to the memory of the author, who, by his sad and premature death, has now silenced for ever all who have criticised his conduct and rejoiced at his fall.

Less than two months before his arrest, Wilde was interviewed for *The Sketch* by a journalist, Gilbert Burgess. The conversation gives a good impression of Wilde at the height of his powers:

On the morning following the production of An Ideal Husband, *I met Oscar Wilde as he came down the steps of a club at the top of St James's Street and I took advantage of the occasion to ask him what he thought of the attitude of the critics towards his play.*

'Well,' *he replied, as he walked slowly down the street,* for a man to be a dramatic critic is as foolish and as inartistic as it would be for a man to be a critic of epics or a pastoral critic, or a critic of lyrics. All modes of art are one, and the modes of the art that employs words as its medium are quite indivisible. The result of the vulgar specialization of criticism is an elaborate scientific knowledge of the stage – almost as elaborate as that of the stage-carpenter and quite on a par with that of the call-boy – combined with an entire incapacity to realize that a play is a work of art, or to receive any artistic impressions at all.'

'*You are rather severe upon dramatic criticism, Mr Wilde.*'

'English dramatic criticism of our own day has never had a single success, in spite of the fact that it goes to all the first nights.'

'*But,*' *I suggested,* '*it is influential.*'

'Certainly, that is why it is so bad.'

'*I don't think I quite . . .* '

'The moment criticism exercises any influence, it ceases to be criticism. The aim of the true critic is to try and chronicle his own moods, not to try and correct the masterpieces of others.'

'*Real critics would be charming in your eyes, then?*'

'Real critics? Ah! how perfectly charming they would be. I am always waiting for their arrival. An inaudible school would be nice. Why do you not found it?'

I was momentarily dazed by the broad vista that had been opened for me, but I retained my presence of mind, and asked: 'Are there absolutely no real critics in London?'

'There are just two.'

'Who are they?' I asked eagerly.

Mr Wilde, with the elaborate courtesy for which he has always been famous, replied, 'I think I had better not mention their names; it might make the others so jealous.'

'What do the literary cliques think of your plays?'

'I don't write to please cliques; I write to please myself. Besides I have always had grave suspicions that the basis of all literary cliques is a morbid love of meat teas. That makes them sadly uncivilized.'

'Still, if your critics offend you, why don't you reply to them?'

'I have far too much time. But I think some day I will give a general answer in the form of a lecture in a public hall which I shall call *Straight Talks to Old Men.*'

'What is your feeling towards your audiences – towards the public?'

'Which public? There are as many publics as there are personalities.'

'Are you nervous on the night that you are producing a new play?'

'Oh, no; I am exquisitely indifferent. My nervousness ends at the last dress rehearsal; I know then what effect my play, as presented on the stage, has produced upon me. My interest in the play ends there, and I feel curiously envious of the public – they have such wonderfully fresh emotions in store for them.'

I laughed, but Mr Wilde rebuked me with a look of surprise.

'It is the public, not the play, that I desire to make a success.'

'But, I'm afraid I don't quite understand – '

'The public makes a success when it realizes that a play is a work of art. On the three first nights I have had in London, the public has been most successful, and, had the dimensions of the stage admitted of it, I would have called them before the curtain. Most managers, I believe, call them behind.'

'I imagine then, that you don't hold with the opinion that the public is the patron of the dramatist?'

'The artist is always the munificent patron of the public. I

am very fond of the public, and, personally, I always patronize
the public very much.'

*'What are your views upon the much-vexed question of subject-matter
in art?'*

'Everything matters in art except the subject.'

*When I recovered, I said, 'Several plays have been written lately that
deal with the monstrous injustice of the social code of morality at the
present time.'*

'Oh,' *answered Mr Wilde, with an air of earnest conviction,* 'it is
indeed a burning shame that there should be one law for men
and another law for women. I think' – *he hesitated, and a smile as
swift as Sterne's 'hectic of a moment' flitted across his face* – 'I think
that there should be no law for anybody.'

*'In writing, do you think that real life or real people should ever give
one inspiration?'*

'The colour of a flower may suggest to one the plot of a
tragedy; a passage in music may give one the sestet of a sonnet;
but whatever actually occurs gives the artist no suggestion.

'Every romance that one has in one's life is a romance lost
to one's art. To introduce real people into a novel or a play
is a sign of an unimaginative mind, a coarse, untutored
observation and an entire absence of style.'

*'I am afraid I can't agree with you, Mr Wilde; I frequently see types
and people who suggest ideas to me.'*

'Everything is of use to the artist except an idea.'

*After that I was silent, until Mr Wilde pointed to the bottom of the
street and drew my attention to the 'apricot-coloured palace' which we
were approaching. So I continued my questioning.*

'The enemy has said that your plays lack action.'

'Yes, English critics always confuse the action of a play with
the incidents of a melodrama. I wrote the first act of *A Woman
of No Importance*, in answer to the critics who said that *Lady
Windermere's Fan* lacked action. In the act of question, there
was absolutely no action at all. It was a perfect act.'

*'What do you think is the chief point that critics have missed in your
new play?'*

'Its entire psychology – the difference in the way in which a
man loves a woman from that in which a woman loves a man;

the passion that women have for making ideals, which is their weakness, and the weakness of a man who dares not show his imperfections to the thing he loves. The end of Act I, and the end of Act II, and the scene in the last act, when Lord Goring points out the higher importance of a man's life over a woman's – to take three prominent instances – seem to have been missed by most of the critics. They failed to see their meaning: they really thought it was a play about a bracelet. We must educate our critics – we must really educate them,' *said Mr Wilde half to himself.*

'The critics subordinate the psychological interest of a play to its mere technique. As soon as a dramatist invents an ingenious situation, they compare him with Sardou, but Sardou is an artist not because of his marvellous instinct of stagecraft, but in spite of it. In the third act of *La Tosca*, the scene of torture, he moved us by a terrible human tragedy, not by his knowledge of stage methods. Sardou is not understood in England because he is only known through a rather ordinary travesty of his play *Dora*, which was brought out here under the title of *Diplomacy*. I have been considerably amused by so many of the critics suggesting that the incident of the diamond bracelet in Act III of my new play was suggested by Sardou. It does not occur in any of Sardou's plays, and it was not in my play until less than ten days before production. Nobody else's work gives me any suggestion. It is only by entire isolation from everything that one can do any work. Idleness gives one the mood in which to write, isolation the conditions. Concentration on one's self recalls the new and wonderful world that one presents in the colour and cadence of words in movement.'

'*And yet we want something more than literature in a play,*' *said I.*

'That is merely because the critics have always propounded the degrading dogma that the duty of the dramatist is to please the public. Rossetti did not weave words into sonnets to please the public, and Corot did not paint silver and grey twilights to please the public. The mere fact of telling any artist to adopt any particular form of art in order to please the public, makes him shun it. We shall never have a real drama in England until it is recognized that a play is as personal and individual a form of self-expression as a poem or a picture.'

'I'm afraid you don't like journalists,' I remarked nervously.

'The journalist is always reminding the public of the existence of the artist. That is unnecessary of him. He is always reminding the artist of the existence of the public. That is indecent of him.'

'But we must have journalists, Mr Wilde.'

'Why? They only record what happens. What does it matter what happens? It is only the abiding things that are interesting, not the horrid incidents of everyday life. Creation for the joy of creation, is the aim of the artist, and that is why the artist is a more divine type than the saint. The artist arrives at his moment with his own mood. He may come with terrible purple tragedies; he may come with dainty rose-coloured comedies – what a charming title!' *added Mr Wilde with a smile –* 'I must write a play and call it *A Rose-Coloured Comedy.*'

'What are the exact relations between literature and the drama?'

'Exquisitely accidental. That is why I think them so necessary.'

'And the exact relations between the actor and the dramatist?'

Mr Wilde looked at me with a serious expression which changed almost immediately into a smile, as he replied, 'Usually a little strained.'

'But surely you regard the actor as a creative artist?'

'Yes,' *replied Mr Wilde with a touch of pathos in his voice,* 'terribly creative – terribly creative!'

'Do you consider that the future outlook of the English stage is hopeful?'

'I think it must be. The critics have ceased to prophesy. That is something. It is in silence that the artist arrives. What is waited for never succeeds; what is heralded is hopeless.'

We were nearing the sentries at Marlborough House, and I said: 'Won't you tell me a little more, please? Let us walk down Pall Mall – exercise is such a good thing.'

'Exercise!' *he ejaculated with an emphasis which almost warrants italics.* 'The only possible form of exercise is to talk, not walk.'

And as he spoke, he motioned to a passing hansom. We shook hands, and Mr Wilde, giving me a glance of approval, said: 'I am sure that you must have a great future in literature before you.'

'What makes you think so?' I asked, as I flushed with pleasure at the prediction.

'Because you seem to be such a very bad interviewer. I feel sure that you must write poetry. I certainly like the colour of your necktie very much. Goodbye.'

'The English Renaissance of Art' was delivered as a lecture for the first time in the Chickering Hall, New York, on 9 January 1882. A portion of it was reported in the *New York Tribune* on the following day and in other American papers subsequently.

There are in existence no fewer than four copies of the lecture, the earliest of which is entirely in the author's handwriting. The others are typewritten and contain many corrections and additions made by the author in manuscript. These have all been collated and the text here given contains, as nearly as possible, the lecture in its original form as delivered by the author during his tour in the United States.

The English
Renaissance of Art

Among the many debts which we owe to the supreme aesthetic faculty of Goethe is that he was the first to teach us to define beauty in terms the most concrete possible, to realize it, I mean, always in its special manifestations. So, in the lecture which I have the honour to deliver before you, I will not try to give you any abstract definition of beauty – any such universal formula for it as was sought for by the philosophy of the eighteenth century – still less to communicate to you that which in its essence is incommunicable, the virtue by which a particular picture or poem affects us with a unique and special joy; but rather to point out to you the general ideas which characterize the great English Renaissance of Art in this century, to discover their source, as far as that is possible, and to estimate their future as far as that is possible.

I call it our English Renaissance because it is indeed a sort of new birth of the spirit of man, like the great Italian Renaissance of the fifteenth century, in its desire for a more gracious and comely way of life, its passion for physical beauty, its exclusive attention to form, its seeking for new subjects for poetry, new forms of art, new intellectual and imaginative enjoyments: and I call it our romantic movement because it is our most recent expression of beauty.

It has been described as a mere revival of Greek modes of thought, and again as a mere revival of mediaeval feeling. Rather I would say that to these forms of the human spirit it has added whatever of artistic value the intricacy and complexity and experience of modern life can give: taking from the one its clearness of vision and its sustained calm, from the other its variety of expression and the mystery of its vision. For what, as Goethe

3

said, is the study of the ancients but a return to the real world (for that is what they did); and what, said Mazzini, is mediaevalism but individuality?

It is really from the union of Hellenism, in its breadth, its sanity of purpose, its calm possession of beauty, with the adventive, the intensified individualism, the passionate colour of the romantic spirit, that springs the art of the nineteenth century in England, as from the marriage of Faust and Helen of Troy sprang the beautiful boy Euphorion.

Such expressions as 'classical' and 'romantic' are, it is true, often apt to become the mere catchwords of schools. We must always remember that art has only one sentence to utter: there is for her only one high law, the law of form or harmony – yet between the classical and romantic spirit we may say that there lies this difference at least, that the one deals with the type and the other with the exception. In the work produced under the modern romantic spirit it is no longer the permanent, the essential truths of life that are treated of; it is the momentary situation of the one, the momentary aspect of the other that art seeks to render. In sculpture, which is the type of one spirit, the subject predominates over the situation; in painting, which is the type of the other, the situation predominates over the subject.

There are two spirits, then: the Hellenic spirit and the spirit of romance may be taken as forming the essential elements of our conscious intellectual tradition, of our permanent standard of taste. As regards their origin, in art as in politics there is but one origin for all revolutions, a desire on the part of man for a nobler form of life, for a freer method and opportunity of expression. Yet, I think that in estimating the sensuous and intellectual spirit which presides over our English Renaissance, any attempt to isolate it in any way from the progress and movement and social life of the age that has produced it would be to rob it of its true vitality, possibly to mistake its true meaning. And in disengaging from the pursuits and passions of this crowded modern world those passions and pursuits which have to do with art and the love of art, we must take into account many great events of history which seem to be the most opposed to any such artistic feeling.

Alien then from any wild, political passion, or from the harsh voice of a rude people in revolt, as our English Renaissance must seem, in its passionate cult of pure beauty, its flawless devotion to form, its exclusive and sensitive nature, it is to the French Revolution that we must look for the most primary factor of its production, the first condition of its birth: that great Revolution of which we are all the children, though the voices of some of us be often loud against it; that Revolution to which at a time when even such spirits as Coleridge and Wordsworth lost heart in England, noble messages of love blown across seas came from your young Republic.

It is true that our modern sense of the continuity of history has shown us that neither in politics nor in nature are there revolutions ever but evolutions only, and that the prelude to that wild storm which swept over France in '89 and made every king in Europe tremble for his throne, was first sounded in literature years before the Bastille fell and the Palace was taken. The way for those red scenes by Seine and Loire was paved by that critical spirit of Germany and England which accustomed men to bring all things to the test of reason or utility or both, while the discontent of the people in the streets of Paris was the echo that followed the life of Émile and of Werther. For Rousseau, by silent lake and mountain, had called humanity back to the golden age that still lies before us and preached a return to nature, in passionate eloquence whose music still lingers about our keen northern air. And Goethe and Scott had brought romance back again from the prison she had lain in for so many centuries – and what is romance but humanity?

Yet in the womb of the Revolution itself, and in the storm and terror of that wild time, tendencies were hidden away that the artistic Renaissance bent to her own service when the time came – a scientific tendency first, which has borne in our own day a brood of somewhat noisy Titans, yet in the sphere of poetry has not been unproductive of good. I do not mean merely in its adding to enthusiasm that intellectual basis which is its strength, or that more obvious influence about which Wordsworth was thinking when he said very nobly that poetry was merely the impassioned expression in the face of science, and that when science would put on a form of flesh and blood the poet would lend his divine spirit to aid the transfiguration. Nor do I dwell much on the great cosmical emotion and deep pantheism of science to which Shelley has given its first and Swinburne its latest glory of song, but rather on its influence on the artistic spirit in preserving that close observation and the sense of limitation as well as of clearness of vision which are the characteristics of the real artist.

The great and golden rule of art as well as of life, wrote William Blake, is that the more distinct, sharp and defined the boundary line, the more perfect is the work of art; and the less keen and sharp the greater is the evidence of weak imitation, plagiarism and bungling. 'Great inventors in all ages knew this – Michelangelo and Albert Dürer are known by this and by this alone'; and another time he wrote, with all the simple directness of nineteenth-century prose, 'to generalize is to be an idiot'.

And this love of definite conception, this clearness of vision, this artistic sense of limit, is the characteristic of all great work and poetry; of the vision of Homer as of the vision of Dante, of Keats and William Morris as of Chaucer and Theocritus. It lies at the base of all noble, realistic and romantic work as opposed to colourless and empty abstractions of our own eighteenth-century poets and of the classical dramatists of France, or of the vague spiritualities of the German sentimental school: opposed, too, to that spirit of transcendentalism which also was root and flower itself of the great Revolution, underlying the impassioned contemplation of Wordsworth and giving wings and fire to the eagle-like flight of Shelley, and which in the sphere of philosophy, though displaced by the materialism and positiveness of our day, bequeathed two great schools of thought, the school of Newman to Oxford, the school of Emerson to America. Yet is this spirit of transcendentalism alien to the spirit of art. For the artist can accept no sphere of life in exchange for life itself. For him there is no escape from the bondage of the earth: there is not even the desire of escape.

He is indeed the only true realist: symbolism, which is the essence of the transcendental spirit, is alien to him. The metaphysical mind of Asia will create for itself the monstrous, many-breasted idol of Ephesus, but to the Greek, pure artist, that work is most instinct with spiritual life which conforms most clearly to the perfect facts of physical life.

'The storm of revolution,' as André Chenier said, 'blows out the torch of poetry.' It is not for some little time that the real influence of such a wild cataclysm of things is felt: at first the desire for equality seems to have produced personalities of more giant and Titan stature than the world had ever known before. Men heard the lyre of Byron and the legions of Napoleon; it was a period of measureless passions and of measureless despair; ambition, discontent, were the chords of life and art; the age was an age of revolt: a phase through which the human spirit must pass but one in which it cannot rest. For the aim of culture is not rebellion but peace, the valley perilous where ignorant armies clash by night being no dwelling-place meet for her to whom the gods have assigned the fresh uplands and sunny heights and clear, untroubled air.

And soon that desire for perfection, which lay at the base of the Revolution, found in a young English poet its most complete and flawless realization.

Phidias and the achievements of Greek art are foreshadowed in Homer: Dante prefigures for us the passion and colour and intensity of Italian painting: the modern love of landscape dates from Rousseau, and it is in Keats that one discerns the beginning of the artistic renaissance of England.

Byron was a rebel and Shelley a dreamer; but in the calmness and clearness of his vision, his perfect self-control, his unerring sense of beauty and his recognition of a separate realm for the imagination, Keats was the pure and serene artist, the forerunner of the pre-Raphaelite school, and so of the great romantic movement of which I am to speak.

Blake had indeed, before him, claimed for art a lofty, spiritual mission, and had striven to raise design to the ideal level of poetry and music, but the remoteness of his vision both in painting and poetry and the incompleteness of his technical powers had been adverse to any real influence. It is in Keats that the artistic spirit of this century first found its absolute incarnation.

And these pre-Raphaelites, what were they? If you ask nine-tenths of the British public what is the meaning of the word aesthetics, they will tell you it is the French for affectation or the German for a dado; and if you inquire about the pre-Raphaelites you will hear something about an eccentric lot of young men to whom a sort of divine crookedness and holy awkwardness in drawing were the chief objects of art. To know nothing about their great men is one of the necessary elements of English education.

As regards the pre-Raphaelites the story is simple enough. In the year 1847 a number of young men in London, poets and painters, passionate admirers of Keats all of them, formed the habit of meeting together for discussions on art, the result of such discussions being that the English Philistine public was roused suddenly from its ordinary apathy by hearing that there was in its midst a body of young men who had determined to revolutionize English painting and poetry. They called themselves the pre-Raphaelite Brotherhood.

In England, then as now, it was enough for a man to try and produce any serious beautiful work to lose all his rights as a citizen; and besides this, the pre-Raphaelite Brotherhood – among whom the names of Dante Rossetti, Holman Hunt and Millais will be familiar to you – had on their side three things that the English public never forgives: youth, power and enthusiasm.

Satire, always as sterile as it is shameful and as impotent as it is insolent, paid them that usual homage which mediocrity pays to genius – doing, here as always, infinite harm to the public, blinding them to what is beautiful, teaching them that irreverence which is the source of all vileness and narrowness of life, but harming the artist not at all, rather confirming him in the perfect rightness of his work and ambition. For to disagree with three-fourths of the British public on all points is one of the first elements of sanity, one of the deepest consolations in all moments of spiritual doubt.

As regards the ideas these young men brought to the regeneration of English art, we may see at the base of their artistic creations a desire for a deeper spiritual value to be given to art as well as a more decorative value.

Pre-Raphaelites they called themselves; not that they imitated the early Italian masters at all, but that in their work, as opposed to the facile abstractions of Raphael, they found a stronger realism of imagination, a more careful realism of technique, a vision at once more fervent and more vivid, an individuality more intimate and more intense.

For it is not enough that a work of art should conform to the aesthetic demands of its age: there must be also about it, if it is to affect us with any permanent delight, the impress of a distinct individuality, an individuality remote from that of ordinary men, and coming near to us only by virtue of a certain newness and wonder in the work, and through channels whose very strangeness makes us more ready to give them welcome.

La personalité, said one of the greatest of modern French critics, *voilà ce qui nous sauvera*.

But above all things was it a return to Nature – that formula which seems to suit so many and such diverse movements: they would draw and paint nothing but what they saw, they would try and imagine things as they really happened. Later there came to the old house by Blackfriars Bridge, where this young brotherhood used to meet and work, two young men from Oxford, Edward Burne-Jones and William Morris – the latter substituting for the simpler realism of the early days a more exquisite spirit of choice, a more faultless devotion to beauty, a more intense seeking for perfection: a master of all exquisite design and of all spiritual vision. It is of the school of Florence rather than of that of Venice that he is kinsman, feeling that the close imitation of Nature is a disturbing element in imaginative art. The visible aspect of modern life disturbs him not; rather is it for him to render eternal all that is beautiful in Greek, Italian and Celtic legend. To Morris we owe poetry whose perfect precision and clearness of word and vision has not been excelled in the literature of our country, and by the revival of the decorative arts he has given to our individualized romantic movement the social idea and the social factor also.

But the revolution accomplished by this clique of young men, with Ruskin's faultless and fervent eloquence to help them, was not one of ideas merely but of execution, not one of conceptions but of creations.

For the great eras in the history of the development of all the arts have been eras not of increased feeling or enthusiasm in feeling for art, but of new technical improvements primarily and specially. The discovery of marble quarries in the purple ravines of Pentelicus and on the little low-lying hills of the island of Paros gave to the Greeks the opportunity for that intensified vitality of action, that more sensuous and simple humanism, to which the Egyptian sculptor working laboriously in the hard porphyry and rose-coloured granite of the desert could not attain. The splendour of the Venetian school began with the introduction of the new oil medium for painting. The progress in modern music has been due to the invention of new instruments entirely, and in no way to an increased consciousness on the part of the musician of any wider social aim. The critic may try and trace the deferred resolutions of Beethoven[1] to some sense of the incompleteness of the modern intellectual spirit, but the artist would have answered, as one of them did afterwards, 'Let them pick out the fifths and leave us at peace.'

And so it is in poetry also: all this love of curious French metres like the Ballade, the Villanelle, the Rondel; all this increased value laid on elaborate alliterations, and on curious words and refrains, such as you will find in Dante Rossetti and Swinburne, is merely the attempt to perfect flute and viol and trumpet through which the spirit of the age and the lips of the poet may blow the music of their many messages.

And so it has been with this romantic movement of ours: it is a reaction against the empty conventional workmanship, the lax execution of previous poetry and painting, showing itself in the work of such men as Rossetti and Burne-Jones by a far greater splendour of colour, a far more intricate wonder of design than English imaginative art has shown before. In Rossetti's poetry and the poetry of Morris, Swinburne and Tennyson a perfect precision and choice of language, a style flawless and fearless, a seeking for all sweet and precious melodies and a sustaining consciousness of the musical value of each word are opposed to

---

[1] As an instance of the inaccuracy of published reports of this lecture, it may be mentioned that previous versions give this passage as *The artist may trace the depressed revolution of Bunthorne simply to the lack of technical means*!

that value which is merely intellectual. In this respect they are
one with the romantic movement of France of which not the least
characteristic note was struck by Théophile Gautier's advice to
the young poet to read his dictionary every day, as being the
only book worth a poet's reading.

While, then, the material of workmanship is being thus elabor-
ated and discovered to have in itself incommunicable and eternal
qualities of its own, qualities entirely satisfying to the poetic
sense and not needing for their aesthetic effect any lofty intellectual vision, any deep criticism of life or even any passionate
human emotion at all, the spirit and the method of the poet's
working – what people call his inspiration – have not escaped
the controlling influence of the artistic spirit. Not that the imagination has lost its wings, but we have accustomed ourselves to
count their innumerable pulsations, to estimate their limitless
strength, to govern their ungovernable freedom.

To the Greeks this problem of the conditions of poetic production, and the places occupied by either spontaneity or self-
consciousness in any artistic work, had a peculiar fascination.
We find it in the mysticism of Plato and in the rationalism of
Aristotle. We find it later in the Italian Renaissance agitating
the minds of such men as Leonardo da Vinci. Schiller tried to
adjust the balance between form and feeling, and Goethe to
estimate the position of self-consciousness in art. Wordsworth's
definition of poetry as 'emotion remembered in tranquillity' may
be taken as an analysis of one of the stages through which all
imaginative work has to pass; and in Keats's longing to be 'able
to compose without this fever' (I quote from one of his letters),
his desire to substitute for poetic ardour 'a more thoughtful and
quiet power', we may discern the most important moment in the
evolution of that artistic life. The question made an early and
strange appearance in your literature too; and I need not remind
you how deeply the young poets of the French romantic movement were excited and stirred by Edgar Allan Poe's analysis of
the workings of his own imagination in the creating of that
supreme imaginative work which we know by the name of *The
Raven*.

In the last century, when the intellectual and didactic element had intruded to such an extent into the kingdom which belongs to poetry, it was against the claims of the understanding that an artist like Goethe had to protest. 'The more incomprehensible to the understanding a poem is the better for it,' he said once, asserting the complete supremacy of the imagination in poetry as of reason in prose. But in this century it is rather against the claims of the emotional faculties, the claims of mere sentiment and feeling, that the artist must react. The simple utterance of joy is not poetry any more than a mere personal cry of pain, and the real experiences of the artist are always those which do not find their direct expression but are gathered up and absorbed into some artistic form which seems, from such real experiences, to be the farthest removed and the most alien.

'The heart contains passion but the imagination alone contains poetry,' says Charles Baudelaire. This too was the lesson that Théophile Gautier, most subtle of all modern critics, most fascinating of all modern poets, was never tired of teaching – 'Everybody is affected by a sunrise or a sunset.' The absolute distinction of the artist is not his capacity to feel nature so much as his power of rendering it. The entire subordination of all intellectual and emotional faculties to the vital and informing poetic principle is the surest sign of the strength of our Renaissance.

We have seen the artistic spirit working, first in the delightful and technical sphere of language, the sphere of expression as opposed to subject, then controlling the imagination of the poet in dealing with his subject. And now I would point out to you its operation in the choice of subject. The recognition of a separate realm for the artist, a consciousness of the absolute difference between the world of art and the world of real fact, between classic grace and absolute reality, forms not merely the essential element of any aesthetic charm but is the characteristic of all great imaginative work and of all great eras of artistic creation – of the age of Phidias as of the age of Michelangelo, of the age of Sophocles as of the age of Goethe.

Art never harms itself by keeping aloof from the social problems of the day: rather, by so doing, it more completely realizes for us that which we desire. For to most of us the real life is the life we do not lead, and thus, remaining more true to the essence of its own perfection, more jealous of its own unattainable beauty, is less likely to forget form in feeling or to accept the passion of creation as any substitute for the beauty of the created thing.

The artist is indeed the child of his own age, but the present will not be to him a whit more real than the past; for, like the philosopher of the Platonic vision, the poet is the spectator of all time and of all existence. For him no form is obsolete, no subject out of date; rather, whatever of life and passion the world has known, in desert of Judaea or in Arcadian valley, by the rivers of Troy or the rivers of Damascus, in the crowded and hideous streets of a modern city or by the pleasant ways of Camelot – all lies before him like an open scroll, all is still instinct with beautiful life. He will take of it what is salutary for his own spirit, no more; choosing some facts and rejecting others with the calm artistic control of one who is in possession of the secret of beauty.

There is indeed a poetical attitude to be adopted towards all things, but all things are not fit subjects for poetry. Into the secure and sacred house of Beauty the true artist will admit nothing that is harsh or disturbing, nothing that gives pain, nothing that is debatable, nothing about which men argue. He can steep himself, if he wishes, in the discussion of all the social problems of his day, poor laws and local taxation, free trade and bimetallic currency, and the like; but when he writes on these subjects it will be, as Milton nobly expressed it, with his left hand, in prose and not in verse, in a pamphlet and not in a lyric. This exquisite spirit of artistic choice was not in Byron: Wordsworth had it not. In the work of both these men there is much that we have to reject, much that does not give us that sense of calm and perfect repose which should be the effect of all fine, imaginative work. But in Keats it seemed to have been incarnate, and in his lovely *Ode on a Grecian Urn* it found its most secure and faultless expression; in the pageant of *The Earthly Paradise* and the knights and ladies of Burne-Jones it is the one dominant note.

It is to no avail that the Muse of Poetry be called, even by such a clarion note as Whitman's, to migrate from Greece and Ionia and to placard REMOVED and TO LET on the rocks of the snowy Parnassus. Calliope's call is not yet closed, nor are the epics of Asia ended; the Sphinx is not yet silent, nor the fountain of Castaly dry. For art is very life itself and knows nothing of death; she is absolute truth and takes no care of fact; she sees (as I remember Mr Swinburne insisting on at dinner) that Achilles is even now more actual and real than Wellington, not merely more noble and interesting as a type and figure but more positive and real.

Literature must rest always on a principle, and temporal considerations are no principle at all. For to the poet all times and places are one; the stuff he deals with is eternal and eternally the same: no theme is inept, no past or present preferable. The steam whistle will not affright him nor the flutes of Arcadia weary him: for him there is but one time, the artistic moment; but one law, the law of form; but one land, the land of Beauty – a land removed indeed from the real world and yet more sensuous because more enduring; calm, yet with that calm which dwells in the faces of the Greek statues, the calm which comes not from the rejection but from the absorption of passion, the calm which despair and sorrow cannot disturb but intensify only. And so it comes that he who seems to stand most remote from his age is he who mirrors it best, because he has stripped life of what is accidental and transitory, stripped it of that 'mist of familiarity which makes life obscure to us.'

Those strange, wild-eyed sibyls fixed eternally in the whirlwind of ecstasy, those mighty-limbed and Titan prophets, labouring with the secret of the earth and the burden of mystery, that guard and glorify the chapel of Pope Sixtus at Rome – do they not tell us more of the real spirit of the Italian Renaissance, of the dream of Savonarola and of the sin of Borgia, than all the brawling boors and cooking women of Dutch art can teach us of the real spirit of the history of Holland?

And so in our own day, also, the two most vital tendencies of the nineteenth century – the democratic and pantheistic tendency and the tendency to value life for the sake of art – found their most complete and perfect utterance in the poetry of Shelley and Keats who, to the blind eyes of their own time, seemed to be as wanderers in the wilderness, preachers of vague or unreal things. And I remember once, in talking to Mr Burne-Jones about modern science, his saying to me, 'the more materialistic science becomes, the more angels shall I paint: their wings are my protest in favour of the immortality of the soul.'

But these are the intellectual speculations that underlie art. Where in the arts themselves are we to find that breadth of human sympathy which is the condition of all noble work; where in the arts are we to look for what Mazzini would call the social ideas as opposed to the merely personal ideas? By virtue of what claim do I demand for the artist the love and loyalty of the men and women of the world? I think I can answer that.

Whatever spiritual message an artist brings to his aid is a matter for his own soul. He may bring judgement like Michelangelo or peace like Angelico; he may come with mourning like the great Athenian or with mirth like the singer of Sicily; nor is it for us to do aught but accept his teaching, knowing that we cannot smite the bitter lips of Leopardi into laughter or burden with our discontent Goethe's serene calm. But for warrant of its truth such message must have the flame of eloquence in the lips that speak it, splendour and glory in the vision that is its witness, being justified by one thing only – the flawless beauty and perfect form of its expression: this indeed being the social idea, being the meaning of joy in art.

Not laughter where none should laugh, nor the calling of peace where there is no peace; not in painting the subject ever, but the pictorial charm only, the wonder of its colour, the satisfying beauty of its design.

You have most of you seen, probably, that great masterpiece of Rubens which hangs in the gallery of Brussels, that swift and wonderful pageant of horse and rider arrested in its most exquisite and fiery moment when the winds are caught in crimson banner and the air lit by the gleam of armour and the flash of plume. Well, that is joy in art, though that golden hillside be trodden by the wounded feet of Christ and it is for the death of the Son of Man that that gorgeous cavalcade is passing.

But this restless modern intellectual spirit of ours is not receptive enough of the sensuous element of art; and so the real influence of the arts is hidden from many of us: only a few, escaping from the tyranny of the soul, have learned the secret of those high hours when thought is not.

And this indeed is the reason of the influence which Eastern art is having on us in Europe, and of the fascination of all Japanese work. While the Western world has been laying on art the intolerable burden of its own intellectual doubts and the spiritual tragedy of its own sorrows, the East has always kept true to art's primary and pictorial conditions.

In judging of a beautiful statue the aesthetic faculty is absolutely and completely gratified by the splendid curves of those marble lips that are dumb to our complaint, the noble modelling of those limbs that are powerless to help us. In its primary aspect a painting has no more spiritual message or meaning than an exquisite fragment of Venetian glass or a blue tile from the wall of Damascus: it is a beautifully coloured surface, nothing more. The channels by which all noble imaginative work in painting should touch, and do touch the soul, are not those of the truths of life, nor metaphysical truths. But that pictorial charm which does not depend on any literary reminiscence for its effect on the one hand, nor is yet a mere result of communicable technical skill on the other, comes of a certain inventive and creative handling of colour. Nearly always in Dutch painting and often in the works of Giorgione or Titian, it is entirely independent of anything definitely poetical in the subject, a kind of form and choice in workmanship which is itself entirely satisfying, and is (as the Greeks would say) an end in itself.

And so in poetry too, the real poetical quality, the joy of poetry, comes never from the subject but from an inventive handling of rhythmical language, from what Keats called the 'sensuous life of verse'. The element of song in the singing accompanied by the profound joy of motion, is so sweet that, while the incomplete lives of ordinary men bring no healing power with them, the thorn-crown of the poet will blossom into roses for our pleasure; for our delight his despair will gild its own thorns, and his pain, like Adonis, be beautiful in its agony; and when the poet's heart breaks it will break in music.

And health in art – what is that? It has nothing to do with a sane criticism of life. There is more health in Baudelaire than there is in Kingsley. Health is the artist's recognition of the limitations of the form in which he works. It is the honour and the homage which he gives to the material he uses – whether it be language with its glories, or marble or pigment with their glories – knowing that the true brotherhood of the arts consists not in their borrowing one another's method, but in their producing, each of them by its own individual means, each of them by keeping its objective limits, the same unique artistic delight. The delight is like that given to us by music – for music is the art in which form and matter are always one, the art whose subject cannot be separated from the method of its expression, the art which most completely realizes the artistic ideal, and is the condition to which all the other arts are constantly aspiring.

And criticism – what place is that to have in our culture? Well, I think that the first duty of an art critic is to hold his tongue at all times, and upon all subjects: *C'est une grande avantage de n'avoir rien fait, mais il ne faut pas en abuser.*

It is only through the mystery of creation that one can gain any knowledge of the quality of created things. You have listened to *Patience* for a hundred nights and you have heard me only for one. It will make, no doubt, that satire more piquant by knowing something about the subject of it, but you must not judge of aestheticism by the satire of Mr Gilbert. As little should you judge of the strength and splendour of the sun or sea by the dust that dances in the beam, or the bubble that breaks on the wave, as take your critic for any sane test of art. For the artists, like the Greek gods, are revealed only to one another, as Emerson says somewhere; their real value and place time only can show. In this respect also omnipotence is with the ages. The true critic addresses not the artist ever but the public only. His work lies with them. Art can never have any other claim but her own perfection: it is for the critic to create for art the social aim, too, by teaching the people the spirit in which they are to approach all artistic work, the love they are to give it, the lesson they are to draw from it.

All these appeals to art to set herself more in harmony with modern progress and civilization, and to make herself the mouthpiece for the voice of humanity, these appeals to art 'to have a mission', are appeals which should be made to the public. The art which has fulfilled the conditions of beauty has fulfilled all conditions: it is for the critic to teach the people how to find in the calm of such art the highest expression of their own most stormy passions. 'I have no reverence,' said Keats, 'for the public, nor for anything in existence but the Eternal Being, the memory of great men and the principle of Beauty.'

Such then is the principle which I believe to be guiding and underlying our English Renaissance, a Renaissance many-sided and wonderful, productive of strong ambitions and lofty personalities, yet for all its splendid achievements in poetry and in the decorative arts and in painting, for all the increased comeliness and grace of dress, and the furniture of houses and the like, not complete. For there can be no great sculpture without a beautiful national life, and the commercial spirit of England has killed that; no great drama without a noble national life, and the commercial spirit of England has killed that too.

It is not that the flawless serenity of marble cannot bear the burden of the modern intellectual spirit, or become instinct with the fire of romantic passion – the tomb of Duke Lorenzo and the chapel of the Medici show us that – but it is that, as Théophile Gautier used to say, the visible world is dead, *le monde visible a disparu.*

Nor is it again that the novel has killed the play, as some critics would persuade us – the romantic movement of France shows us that. The work of Balzac and of Hugo grew up side by side together; nay, more, were complementary to each other, though neither of them saw it. While all other forms of poetry may flourish in an ignoble age, the splendid individualism of the lyrist, fed by its own passion, and lit by its own power, may pass as a pillar of fire as well across the desert as across places that are pleasant. It is none the less glorious though no man follow it – nay, by the greater sublimity of its loneliness it may be quickened into loftier utterance and intensified into clearer song. From the mean squalor of the sordid life that limits him, the dreamer or the idyllist may soar on poesy's viewless wings, may traverse with fawn-skin and spear the moonlit heights of Cithaeron though Faun and Bassarid dance there no more. Like

Keats he may wander through the old-world forests of Latmos, or stand like Morris on the galley's deck with the Viking when king and galley have long since passed away. But the drama is the meeting-place of art and life; it deals, as Mazzini said, not merely with man, but with social man, with man in his relation to God and to Humanity. It is the product of a period of great national united energy; it is impossible without a noble public, and belongs to such ages as the age of Elizabeth in London and of Pericles at Athens; it is part of such lofty moral and spiritual ardour as came to Greek after the defeat of the Persian fleet, and to Englishman after the wreck of the Armada of Spain.

Shelley felt how incomplete our movement was in this respect, and has shown in one great tragedy by what terror and pity he would have purified our age; but in spite of *The Cenci* the drama is one of the artistic forms through which the genius of the England of this century seeks in vain to find outlet and expression. He has had no worthy imitators.

It is rather, perhaps, to you that we should turn to complete and perfect this great movement of ours, for there is something Hellenic in your air and world, something that has a quicker breath of the joy and power of Elizabeth's England about it than our ancient civilization can give us. For you, at least, are young; 'no hungry generations tread you down,' and the past does not weary you with the intolerable burden of its memories nor mock you with the ruins of a beauty, the secret of whose creation you have lost. That very absence of tradition, which Mr Ruskin thought would rob your rivers of their laughter and your flowers of their light, may be rather the source of your freedom and your strength.

To speak in literature with the perfect rectitude and insouciance of the movements of animals, and the unimpeachableness of the sentiment of trees in the woods and grass by the roadside, has been defined by one of your poets as a flawless triumph of art. It is a triumph which you above all nations may be destined to achieve. For the voices that have their dwelling in sea and mountain are not the chosen music of Liberty only; other messages are there in the wonder of wind-swept height and the majesty of silent deep – messages that, if you will but listen to them, may yield you the splendour of some new imagination, the marvel of some new beauty.

'I foresee,' said Goethe, 'the dawn of a new literature which all people may claim as their own, for all have contributed to its foundation.' If, then, this is so, and if the materials for a civilization as great as that of Europe lie all around you, what profit, you will ask me, will all this study of our poets and painters be to you? I might answer that the intellect can be engaged without direct didactic object on an artistic and historical problem; that the demand of the intellect is merely to feel itself alive; that nothing which has ever interested men or women can cease to be a fit subject for culture.

I might remind you of what all Europe owes to the sorrow of a single Florentine in exile at Verona, or to the love of Petrarch by that little well in Southern France; nay, more, how even in this dull, materialistic age the simple expression of an old man's simple life, passed away from the clamour of great cities amid the lakes and misty hills of Cumberland, has opened out for England treasures of new joy compared with which the treasures of her luxury are as barren as the sea which she has made her highway, and as bitter as the fire which she would make her slave.

But I think it will bring you something besides this, something that is the knowledge of real strength in art: not that you should imitate the works of these men; but their artistic spirit, their artistic attitude, I think you should absorb that.

For in nations, as in individuals, if the passion for creation be not accompanied by the critical, the aesthetic faculty also, it will be sure to waste its strength aimlessly, failing perhaps in the artistic spirit of choice, or in the mistaking of feeling for form, or in the following of false ideals.

For the various spiritual forms of the imagination have a natural affinity with certain sensuous forms of art – and to discern the qualities of each art, to intensify as well its limitations as its powers of expression, is one of the aims that culture sets before us. It is not an increased moral sense, an increased moral supervision that your literature needs. Indeed, one should never talk of a moral or an immoral poem – poems are either well written or badly written, that is all. And, indeed, any element of morals or implied reference to a standard of good or evil in art is often a sign of a certain incompleteness of vision, often a note of discord in the harmony of an imaginative creation; for all good work aims at a purely artistic effect. 'We must be careful,' said Goethe, 'not to be always looking for culture merely in what is obviously moral. Everything that is great promotes civilization as soon as we are aware of it.'

But, as in your cities so in your literature, it is a permanent canon and standard of taste, an increased sensibility to beauty (if I may say so) that is lacking. All noble work is not national merely, but universal. The political independence of a nation must not be confused with any intellectual isolation. The spiritual freedom, indeed, your own generous lives and liberal air will give you. From us you will learn the classical restraint of form.

For all great art is delicate art, roughness having very little to do with strength, and harshness very little to do with power. 'The artist,' as Mr Swinburne says, 'must be perfectly articulate.'

This limitation is for the artist perfect freedom: it is at once the origin and the sign of his strength. So that all the supreme masters of style – Dante, Sophocles, Shakespeare – are the supreme masters of spiritual and intellectual vision also.

Love art for its own sake, and then all things that you need will be added to you.

This devotion to beauty and to the creation of beautiful things is the test of all great civilized nations. Philosophy may teach us to bear with equanimity the misfortunes of our neighbours, and science resolve the moral sense into a secretion of sugar, but art is what makes the life of each citizen a sacrament and not a speculation, art is what makes the life of the whole race immortal.

For beauty is the only thing that time cannot harm. Philosophies fall away like sand, and creeds follow one another like the withered leaves of autumn; but what is beautiful is a joy for all seasons and a possession for all eternity.

Wars and the clash of armies and the meeting of men in battle by trampled field or leaguered city, and the rising of nations there must always be. But I think that art, by creating a common intellectual atmosphere between all countries, might – if it could not overshadow the world with the silver wings of peace – at least make men such brothers that they would not go out to slay one another for the whim or folly of some king or minister, as they do in Europe. Fraternity would come no more with the hands of Cain, nor Liberty betray freedom with the kiss of Anarchy; for national hatreds are always strongest where culture is lowest.

'How could I?' said Goethe, when reproached for not writing like Korner against the French. 'How could I, to whom barbarism and culture alone are of importance, hate a nation which is among the most cultivated of the earth, a nation to which I owe a great part of my own cultivation?'

Mighty empires, too, there must always be as long as personal ambition and the spirit of the age are one, but art at least is the only empire which a nation's enemies cannot take from her by conquest, but which is taken by submission only. The sovereignty of Greece and Rome is not yet passed away, though the gods of the one be dead and the eagles of the other tired.

And we in our Renaissance are seeking to create a sovereignty that will still be England's when her yellow leopards have grown weary of wars and the rose of her shield is crimsoned no more with the blood of battle; and you, too, absorbing into the generous heart of a great people this pervading artistic spirit, will create for yourselves such riches as you have never yet created, though your land be a network of railways and your cities the harbours for the galleys of the world.

I know, indeed, that the divine natural prescience of beauty which is the inalienable inheritance of Greek and Italian is not our inheritance. For such an informing and presiding spirit of art to shield us from all harsh and alien influences, we of the Northern races must turn rather to that strained self-consciousness of our age which, as it is the keynote of all our romantic art, must be the source of all or nearly all our culture. I mean that intellectual curiosity of the nineteenth century which is always looking for the secret of the life that still lingers round old and bygone forms of culture. It takes from each what is serviceable for the modern spirit – from Athens its wonder without its worship, from Venice its splendour without its sin. The same spirit is always analysing its own strength and its own weakness, counting what it owes to East and to West, to the olive trees of Colonus and to the palm trees of Lebanon, to Gethsemane and to the gardens of Proserpine.

And yet the truths of art cannot be taught: they are revealed only, revealed to natures which have made themselves receptive of all beautiful impressions by the study and worship of all beautiful things. And hence the enormous importance given to the decorative arts in our English Renaissance; hence all that marvel of design that comes from the hand of Edward Burne-Jones, all that weaving of tapestry and staining of glass, that beautiful working in clay and metal and wood which we owe to William Morris, the greatest handicraftsman we have had in England since the fourteenth century.

So, in years to come there will be nothing in any man's house which has not given delight to its maker and does not give delight to its user. The children, like the children of Plato's perfect city, will grow up 'in a simple atmosphere of all fair things' – I quote from the passage in the *Republic* – 'a simple atmosphere of all fair things, where beauty, which is the spirit of art, will come on eye and ear like a fresh breath of wind that brings health from a clear upland, and insensibly and gradually draw the child's soul into harmony with all knowledge and all wisdom, so that he will love what is beautiful and good, and hate what is evil and ugly (for they always go together) long before he knows the reason why; and then when reason comes will kiss her on the cheek as a friend.'

That is what Plato thought decorative art could do for a nation, feeling that the secret not of philosophy merely but of all gracious existence might be externally hidden from any one whose youth had been passed in uncomely and vulgar surroundings, and that the beauty of form and colour even, as he says, in the meanest vessels of the house, will find its way into the inmost places of the soul and lead the boy naturally to look for that divine harmony of spiritual life of which art was to him the material symbol and warrant.

Prelude indeed to all knowledge and all wisdom will this love of beautiful things be for us; yet there are times when wisdom becomes a burden and knowledge is one with sorrow: for as every body has its shadow so every soul has its scepticism. In such dread moments of discord and despair where should we, of this torn and troubled age, turn our steps if not to that secure house of beauty where there is always a little forgetfulness, always a great joy; to that *città divina*, as the old Italian heresy called it, the divine city where one can stand, though only for a brief moment, apart from the division and terror of the world and the choice of the world too?

This is that *consolation des arts* which is the keynote of Gautier's poetry, the secret of modern life foreshadowed – as indeed what in our century is not? – by Goethe. You remember what he said to the German people: 'Only have the courage,' he said, 'to give yourselves up to your impressions, allow yourselves to be delighted, moved, elevated, nay instructed, inspired for something great.' The courage to give yourselves up to your impressions: yes, that is the secret of the artistic life – for while art has been defined as an escape from the tyranny of the senses, it is an escape rather from the tyranny of the soul. But only to those who worship her above all things does she ever reveal her true treasure: else will she be as powerless to aid you as the mutilated Venus of the Louvre was before the romantic but sceptical nature of Heine.

And indeed I think it would be impossible to overrate the gain that might follow if we had about us' only what gave pleasure to the maker of it and gives pleasure to its user, that being the simplest of all rules about decoration. One thing, at least, I think it would do for us: there is no surer test of a great country than how near it stands to its own poets; but between the singers of our day and the workers to whom they would sing there seems to be an ever-widening and dividing chasm, a chasm which slander and mockery cannot traverse, but which is spanned by the luminous wings of love.

And of such love I think that the abiding presence in our houses of noble imaginative work would be the surest seed and preparation. I do not mean merely as regards that direct literary expression of art by which, from the little red-and-black cruse of oil or wine, a Greek boy could learn of the lionlike splendour of

Achilles, of the strength of Hector and the beauty of Paris and the wonder of Helen, long before he stood and listened in crowded market-place or in theatre of marble; or by which an Italian child of the fifteenth century could know of the chastity of Lucrece and the death of Camilla from carven doorway and from painted chest. For the good we get from art is not what we learn from it; it is what we become through it. Its real influence will be in giving the mind that enthusiasm which is the secret of Hellenism, accustoming it to demand from art all that art can do in rearranging the facts of common life for us – whether it be by giving the most spiritual interpretation of one's own moments of highest passion or the most sensuous expression of those thoughts that are the farthest removed from sense; in accustoming it to love the things of the imagination for their own sake, and to desire beauty and grace in all things. For he who does not love art in all things does not love it at all, and he who does not need art in all things does not need it at all.

I will not dwell here on what I am sure has delighted you all in our great Gothic cathedrals. I mean how the artist of that time, handicraftsman himself in stone or glass, found the best motives for his art, always ready for his hand and always beautiful, in the daily work of the artificers he saw around him – as in those lovely windows of Chartres – where the dyer dips in the vat and the potter sits at the wheel, and the weaver stands at the loom: real manufacturers these, workers with the hand, and entirely delightful to look at, not like the smug and vapid shopman of our time, who knows nothing of the web or vase he sells, except that he is charging you double its value and thinking you a fool for buying it. Nor can I but just note, in passing, the immense influence the decorative work of Greece and Italy had on its artists, the one teaching the sculptor that restraining influence of design which is the glory of the Parthenon, the other keeping painting always true to its primary, pictorial condition of noble colour which is the secret of the school of Venice; for I wish rather, in this lecture at least, to dwell on the effect that decorative art has on human life – on its social not its purely artistic effect.

There are two kinds of men in the world, two great creeds,

two different forms of natures: men to whom the end of life is action, and men to whom the end of life is thought. As regards the latter, who seek for experience itself and not for the fruits of experience, who must burn always with one of the passions of this fiery-coloured world, who find life interesting not for its secret but for its situations, for its pulsations and not for its purpose; the passion for beauty engendered by the decorative arts will be to them more satisfying than any political or religious enthusiasm, any enthusiasm for humanity, any ecstasy or sorrow for love. For art comes to one professing primarily to give nothing but the highest quality to one's moments, and for those moments' sake. So far for those to whom the end of life is thought. As regards the others, who hold that life is inseparable from labour, to them should this movement be specially dear: for, if our days are barren without industry, industry without art is barbarism.

Hewers of wood and drawers of water there must be always indeed among us. Our modern machinery has not much lightened the labour of man after all: but at least let the pitcher that stands by the well be beautiful and surely the labour of the day will be lightened: let the wood be made receptive of some lovely form, some gracious design, and there will come no longer discontent but joy to the toiler. For what is decoration but the worker's expression of joy in his work? And not joy merely – that is a great thing yet not enough – but that opportunity of expressing his own individuality which, as it is the essence of all life, is the source of all art. 'I have tried,' I remember William Morris saying to me once, 'I have tried to make each of my workers an artist, and when I say an artist I mean a man.' For the worker then, handicraftsman of whatever kind he is, art is no longer to be a purple robe woven by a slave and thrown over the whitened body of a leprous king to hide and to adorn the sin of his luxury, but rather the beautiful and noble expression of a life that has in it something beautiful and noble.

And so you must seek out your workman and give him, as far as possible, the right surroundings, for remember that the real test and virtue of a workman is not his earnestness nor his industry even, but his power of design merely; and that 'design is not the offspring of idle fancy: it is the studied result of accumulative observation and delightful habit.' All the teaching in the world is of no avail if you do not surround your workman with happy influences and with beautiful things. It is impossible for him to have right ideas about colour unless he sees the lovely colours of Nature unspoiled; impossible for him to supply beautiful incident and action unless he sees beautiful incident and action in the world about him.

For to cultivate sympathy you must be among living things and thinking about them, and to cultivate admiration you must be among beautiful things and looking at them. 'The steel of Toledo and the silk of Genoa did but give strength to oppression and lustre to pride,' as Mr Ruskin says; let it be for you to create an art that is made by the hands of the people for the joy of the people, to please the hearts of the people, too; an art that will be your expression of your delight in life. There is nothing 'in common life too mean, in common things too trivial to be ennobled by your touch'; nothing in life that art cannot sanctify.

You have heard, I think, a few of you, of two flowers connected with the aesthetic movement in England, and said (I assure you, erroneously) to be the food of some aesthetic young men. Well, let me tell you that the reason we love the lily and the sunflower, in spite of what Mr Gilbert may tell you, is not for any vegetable fashion at all. It is because these two lovely flowers are in England the two most perfect models of design, the most naturally adapted for decorative art – the gaudy leonine beauty of the one and the precious loveliness of the other giving to the artist the most entire and perfect joy. And so with you: let there be no flower in your meadows that does not wreathe its tendrils around your pillows, no little leaf in your Titan forests that does not lend its form to design, no curving spray of wild rose or brier that does not live for ever in carven arch or window or marble, no bird in your air that is not giving the iridescent wonder of its colour, the exquisite curves of its wings in flight, to make more precious the preciousness of simple adornment. For the voices that have their dwelling in sea and mountain are not the chosen music of liberty only. Other messages are there in the wonder of windswept heights and the majesty of silent deep – messages that, if you will listen to them, will give you the wonder of all new imagination, the treasure of all new beauty.

We spend our days, each one of us, in looking for the secret of life. Well, the secret of life is in art.

London Models

English Illustrated Magazine, January 1889

Professional models are a purely modern invention. To the Greeks, for instance, they were quite unknown. Mr Mahaffy, it is true, tells us that Pericles used to present peacocks to the great ladies of Athenian society in order to induce them to sit to his friend Phidias, and we know that Polygnotus introduced into his picture of the Trojan women the face of Elpinice, the celebrated sister of the great Conservative leader of the day, but these *grandes dames* clearly do not come under our category. As for the old masters, they undoubtedly made constant studies from their pupils and apprentices, and even their religious pictures are full of the portraits of their friends and relations, but they do not seem to have had the inestimable advantage of the existence of a class of people whose sole profession is to pose. In fact the model, in our sense of the word, is the direct creation of Academic Schools.

Every country now has its own models, except America. In New York, and even in Boston, a good model is so great a rarity that most of the artists are reduced to painting Niagara and millionaires. In Europe, however, it is different. Here we have plenty of models, and of every nationality. The Italian models are the best. The natural grace of their attitudes, as well as the wonderful picturesqueness of their colouring, makes them facile – often too facile – subjects for the painter's brush. The French models, though not so beautiful as the Italian, possess a quickness of intellectual sympathy, a capacity, in fact, of understanding the artist, which is quite remarkable. They have also a great command over the varieties of facial expression, are peculiarly dramatic, and can chatter the *argot* of the *atelier* as cleverly as the critic of the *Gil Blas*. The English models form a class entirely by themselves. They are not so picturesque as the Italian, nor so clever as the French, and they have absolutely no tradition, so to speak, of their order. Now and then some old veteran knocks at a studio door, and proposes to sit as Ajax defying the lightning, or as King Lear upon the blasted heath. One of them some time ago called on a popular painter who, happening at the moment to require his services, engaged him, and told him to begin by kneeling down in the attitude of prayer. 'Shall I be Biblical or Shakespearean, sir?' asked the veteran. 'Well – Shakespearean,' answered the artist, wondering by what subtle *nuance* of expression the model would convey the difference. 'All right, sir,' said the professor of posing, and he solemnly knelt down and began to wink with his left eye! This class, however, is dying out. As a rule the model, nowadays, is a pretty girl, from about twelve to twenty-five years of age, who knows nothing about art, cares less, and is merely anxious to earn seven or eight shillings a day without much trouble. English models rarely look at a picture, and never venture on any aesthetic theories. In fact, they realize very completely Mr Whistler's idea of the function of an art critic, for they pass no criticisms at all. They accept all schools of art with the grand catholicity of the auctioneer, and sit to a fantastic young impressionist as readily as to a learned and laborious academician. They are neither for the Whistlerites nor against them; the quarrel between the school of facts and the school of effects touches them not; idealistic and naturalistic are words that convey no meaning to their ears; they merely desire that the studio shall be warm, and the lunch hot, for all charming artists give their models lunch.

As to what they are asked to do they are equally indifferent. On Monday they will don the rags of a beggar-girl for Mr Pumper, whose pathetic pictures of modern life draw such tears from the public, and on Tuesday they will pose in a peplum for Mr Phoebus, who thinks that all really artistic subjects are necessarily BC. They career gaily through all centuries and through all costumes, and, like actors, are interesting only when they are not themselves. They are extremely good-natured, and very accommodating. 'What do you sit for?' said a young artist to a model who had sent him in her card (all models, by the way, have cards and a small black bag). 'Oh, for anything you like, sir,' said the girl, 'landscape if necessary!'

Intellectually, it must be acknowledged, they are Philistines, but physically they are perfect – at least some are. Though none of them can talk Greek, many can look Greek, which to a nineteenth-century painter is naturally of great importance. If they are allowed, they chatter a great deal, but they never say anything. Their observations are the only *banalités* heard in Bohemia. However, though they cannot appreciate the artist as artist, they are quite ready to appreciate the artist as a man. They are very sensitive to kindness, respect and generosity. A beautiful model who had sat for two years to one of our most distinguished English painters, got engaged to a street vendor of penny ices. On her marriage the painter sent her a pretty wedding present, and received in return a nice letter of thanks with the following remarkable postscript: 'Never eat the green ices!'

When they are tired a wise artist gives them a rest. Then they sit in a chair and read penny dreadfuls, till they are roused from the tragedy of literature to take their place again in the tragedy of art. A few of them smoke cigarettes. This, however, is regarded by the other models as showing a want of seriousness, and is not generally approved of. They are engaged by the day and by the half day. The tariff is a shilling an hour, to which great artists usually add an omnibus fare. The two best things about them are their extraordinary prettiness, and their extreme respectability. As a class they are very well behaved, particularly those who sit for the figure, a fact which is curious or natural according to the view one takes of human nature. They usually marry well, and sometimes they marry the artist. For an artist to marry his model is as fatal as for a *gourmet* to marry his cook: the one gets no sittings, and the other gets no dinners.

On the whole the English female models are very naïve, very natural and very good-humoured. The virtues which the artist values most in them are prettiness and punctuality. Every sensible model consequently keeps a diary of her engagements, and dresses neatly. The bad season is, of course, the summer, when the artists are out of town. However, of late years some artists have engaged their models to follow them, and the wife of one of our most charming painters has often had three or four models under her charge in the country, so that the work of her husband and his friends should not be interrupted. In France the models migrate *en masse* to the little seaport villages or forest hamlets where the painters congregate. The English models, however, wait patiently in London, as a rule, till the artists come back. Nearly all of them live with their parents, and help to support the house. They have every qualification for being immortalized in art except that of beautiful hands. The hands of the English model are nearly always coarse and red.

As for the male models, there is the veteran whom we have mentioned above. He has all the traditions of the grand style, and is rapidly disappearing with the school he represents. An old man who talks about Fuseli is, of course, unendurable, and, besides, patriarchs have ceased to be fashionable subjects. Then there is the true Academy model. He is usually a man of thirty, rarely good-looking, but a perfect miracle of muscles. In fact he is the apotheosis of anatomy, and is so conscious of his own splendour that he tells you of his tibia and his thorax, as if no one else had anything of the kind. Then come the Oriental models. The supply of these is limited, but there are always about a dozen in London. They are very much sought after as they can remain immobile for hours, and generally possess lovely costumes. However, they have a very poor opinion of English art, which they regard as something between a vulgar personality and a commonplace photograph. Next we have the Italian youth who has come over specially to be a model, or takes to it when his organ is out of repair. He is often quite charming with his large melancholy eyes, his crisp hair, and his slim brown figure. It is true he eats garlic, but then he can stand like a faun and couch like a leopard, so he is forgiven. He is always full of pretty compliments, and has been known to have kind words of encouragement for even our greatest artists. As for the English lad of the same age, he never sits at all. Apparently he does not regard the career of a model as a serious profession. In any case he is rarely, if ever, to be got hold of. English boys, too, are difficult to find. Sometimes an ex-model who has a son will curl his hair, and wash his face, and bring him the round of the studios, all soap and shininess. The young school don't like him, but the older school do, and when he appears on the walls of the Royal Academy he is called *The Infant Samuel*. Occasionally also an artist catches a couple of *gamins* in the gutter and asks them to come to his studio. The first time they always appear, but after that they don't keep their appointments. They dislike sitting still, and have a strong and perhaps natural objection to looking pathetic. Besides, they are always under the impression that the artist is laughing at them. It is a sad fact, but there is no doubt that the poor are completely unconscious of their own picturesqueness. Those of them who can be induced to sit do so with the idea that the artist is merely a benevolent philanthropist who has chosen an eccentric method of distributing alms to the undeserving. Perhaps the School Board will teach the London *gamin* his own artistic value, and then they will be better models than they are now. One remarkable privilege belongs to the Academy model, that of extorting a sovereign from any newly elected Associate or RA. They wait at Burlington House till the announcement is made, and then race to the hapless artist's house. The one who arrives first receives the money. They have of late been much troubled at the long distances they have had to run, and they look with disfavour on the election of artists who live at Hampstead or at Bedford Park, for it is considered a point of honour not to employ the underground railway, omnibuses, or any artificial means of locomotion. The race is to the swift.

Besides the professional posers of the studio there are posers of the Row, the posers at afternoon teas, the posers in politics and the circus posers. All four classes are delightful, but only the last class is ever really decorative. Acrobats and gymnasts can give the young painter infinite suggestions, for they bring into their art an element of swiftness of motion and of constant change that the studio model necessarily lacks. What is interesting in these 'slaves of the ring' is that with them Beauty is an unconscious result not a conscious aim, the result in fact of the mathematical calculation of curves and distances, of absolute precision of eye, of the scientific knowledge of the equilibrium of forces, and of perfect physical training. A good acrobat is always graceful, though grace is never his object; he is graceful because he does what he has to do in the best way in which it can be done – graceful because he is natural. If an ancient Greek were to come to life now, which considering the probable severity of his criticisms would be rather trying to our conceit, he would be found far oftener at the circus than at the theatre. A good circus is an oasis of Hellenism in a world that reads too much to be wise, and thinks too much to be beautiful. If it were not for the running-ground at Eton, the towing-path at Oxford, the Thames swimming-baths, and the yearly circuses, humanity would forget the plastic perfection of its own form, and degenerate into a race of short-sighted professors and spectacled *précieuses*. Not that the circus proprietors are, as a rule, conscious of their high mission. Do they not bore us with the *haute école*, and weary us with Shakespearean clowns? Still, at least, they give us acrobats, and the acrobat is an artist. The mere fact that he never speaks to the audience shows how well he appreciates the great truth that the aim of art is not to reveal personality but to please. The clown may be blatant, but the acrobat is always beautiful. He is an interesting combination of the spirit of Greek sculpture with the spangles of the modern costumier. He has even had his niche in the novels of our age, and if *Manette Salomon* be the unmasking of the model, *Les Frères Zemganno* is the apotheosis of the acrobat.

As regards the influence of the ordinary model on our English school of painting, it cannot be said that it is altogether good. It is, of course, an advantage for the young artist sitting in his studio to be able to isolate 'a little corner of life', as the French say, from disturbing surroundings, and to study it under certain effects of light and shade. But this very isolation leads often to mere mannerism in the painter, and robs him of that broad acceptance of the general facts of life which is the very essence of art. Model-painting, in a word, while it may be the condition of art, is not by any means its aim. It is simply practice, not perfection. Its use trains the eye and the hand of the painter, its abuse produces in his work an effect of mere posing and pretti-ness. It is the secret of much of the artificiality of modern art, this constant posing of pretty people, and when art becomes artificial it becomes monotonous. Outside the little world of the studio, with its draperies and its *bric-à-brac*, lies the world of life with its infinite, its Shakespearean variety. We must, however, distinguish between the two kinds of models, those who sit for the figure and those who sit for the costume. The study of the first is always excellent, but the costume-model is becoming rather wearisome in modern pictures. It is really of very little use to dress up a London girl in Greek draperies and to paint her as a goddess. The robe may be the robe of Athens, but the face is usually the face of Brompton. Now and then, it is true, one comes across a model whose face is an exquisite anachronism, and who looks lovely and natural in the dress of any century but her own. This, however, is rather rare. As a rule models are absolutely *de notre siècle*, and should be painted as such. Unfortunately they are not, and, as a consequence, we are shown every year a series of scenes from fancy dress balls which are called historical pictures, but are little more than mediocre representations of modern people masquerading. In France they are wiser. The French painter uses the model simply for study; for the finished picture he goes direct to life.

However, we must not blame the sitters for the shortcomings of the artists. The English models are a well-behaved and hardworking class, and if they are more interested in artists than in art, a large section of the public is in the same condition, and most of our modern exhibitions seem to justify its choice.

The American Invasion

Court and Society Review, 23 March 1887

A terrible danger is hanging over the Americans in London. Their future and their reputation this season depend entirely on the success of Buffalo Bill and Mrs Brown-Potter. The former is certain to draw; for English people are far more interested in American barbarism than they are in American civilization. When they sight Sandy Hook they look to their rifles and ammunition; and, after dining once at Delmonico's, start off for Colorado or California, for Montana or the Yellowstone Park. Rocky Mountains charm them more than riotous millionaires; they have been known to prefer buffaloes to Boston. Why should they not? The cities of America are inexpressibly tedious. The Bostonians take their learning too sadly; culture with them is an accomplishment rather than an atmosphere; their 'Hub', as they call it, is the paradise of prigs. Chicago is a sort of monster-shop, full of bustle and bores. Political life at Washington is like political life in a suburban vestry. Baltimore is amusing for a week, but Philadelphia is dreadfully provincial; and though one can dine in New York one could not dwell there. Better the Far West with its grizzly bears and its untamed cowboys, its free open-air life and its free open-air manners, its boundless prairie and its boundless mendacity! This is what Buffalo Bill is going to bring to London; and we have no doubt that London will fully appreciate his show.

With regard to Mrs Brown-Potter, as acting is no longer considered absolutely essential for success on the English stage, there is really no reason why the pretty bright-eyed lady who charmed us all last June by her merry laugh and her nonchalant ways, should not – to borrow an expression from her native language – make a big boom and paint the town red. We sincerely hope she will; for, on the whole, the American invasion has done English society a great deal of good. American women are bright, clever, and wonderfully cosmopolitan. Their patriotic feelings are limited to an admiration for Niagara and a regret for the Elevated Railway; and, unlike the men, they never bore us with Bunkers Hill. They take their dresses from Paris and their manners from Piccadilly, and wear both charmingly. They have a quaint pertness, a delightful conceit, a native self-assertion. They insist on being paid compliments and have almost succeeded in making Englishmen eloquent. For our aristocracy they have an ardent admiration; they adore titles and are a permanent blow to Republican principles. In the art of amusing men they are adepts, both by nature and education, and can actually tell a story without forgetting the point – an accomplishment that is extremely rare among the women of other countries. It is true that they lack repose and that their voices are somewhat harsh and strident when they land first at Liverpool; but after a time one gets to love these pretty whirlwinds in petticoats that sweep so recklessly through society and are so agitating to all duchesses who have daughters. There is something fascinating in their funny, exaggerated gestures and their petulant way of tossing the head. Their eyes have no magic nor mystery in them, but they challenge us for combat; and when we engage we are always worsted. Their lips seem made for laughter and yet they never grimace. As for their voices, they soon get them into tune. Some of them have been known to acquire a fashionable drawl in two seasons; and after they have been presented to Royalty they all roll their Rs as vigorously as a young equerry or an old lady-in-waiting. Still, they never really lose their accent: it keeps peeping out here and there, and when they chatter together they are like a bevy of peacocks. Nothing is more amusing than to watch two American girls greeting each other in a drawing-room or in the Row. They are like children with their shrill staccato cries of wonder, their odd little exclamations. Their conversation sounds like a series of exploding crackers; they are exquisitely incoherent and use a sort of primitive, emotional language. After five minutes they are left beautifully breathless and look at each other half in amusement and half in affection. If a stolid young

Englishman is fortunate enough to be introduced to them he is amazed at their extraordinary vivacity, their electric quickness of repartee, their inexhaustible store of curious catchwords. He never really understands them, for their thoughts flutter about with the sweet irresponsibility of butterflies; but he is pleased and amused and feels as if he were in an aviary. On the whole, American girls have a wonderful charm and, perhaps, the chief secret of their charm is that they never talk seriously except about amusements. They have, however, one grave fault – their mothers. Dreary as were those old Pilgrim Fathers who left our shores more than two centuries ago to found a New England beyond seas, the Pilgrim Mothers who have returned to us in the nineteenth century are drearier still.

Here and there, of course, there are exceptions, but as a class they are either dull, dowdy or dyspeptic. It is only fair to the rising generation of America to state that they are not to blame for this. Indeed, they spare no pains at all to bring up their parents properly and to give them a suitable, if somewhat late, education. From its earliest years every American child spends most of its time in correcting the faults of its father and mother; and no one who has had the opportunity of watching an American family on the deck of an Atlantic steamer, or in the refined seclusion of a New York boarding-house, can fail to have been struck by this characteristic of their civilization. In America the young are always ready to give to those who are older than themselves the full benefits of their inexperience. A boy of only eleven or twelve years of age will firmly but kindly point out to his father his defects of manner or temper; will never weary of warning him against extravagance, idleness, late hours, unpunctuality, and the other temptations to which the aged are so particularly exposed; and sometimes, should he fancy that he is monopolizing too much of the conversation at dinner, will remind him, across the table, of the new child's adage, 'Parents should be seen, not heard.' Nor does any mistaken idea of kindness prevent the little American girl from censuring her mother whenever it is necessary. Often, indeed, feeling that a rebuke conveyed in the presence of others is more truly efficacious than one merely whispered in the quiet of the nursery, she will call the attention of perfect strangers to her mother's general untidiness, her want of intellectual Boston conversation, immoderate love of iced water and green corn, stinginess in the matter of candy, ignorance of the usages of the best Baltimore society, bodily ailments and the like. In fact, it may be truly said that no American child is ever blind to the deficiencies of its parents, no matter how much it may love them.

Yet, somehow, this educational system has not been so successful as it deserved. In many cases, no doubt, the material with which the children had to deal was crude and incapable of real development; but the fact remains that the American mother is a tedious person. The American father is better, for he is never seen in London. He passes his life entirely in Wall Street and communicates with his family once a month by means of a telegram in cipher. The mother, however, is always with us, and, lacking the quick imitative faculty of the younger generation, remains uninteresting and provincial to the last. In spite of her, however, the American girl is always welcome. She brightens our dull dinner parties for us and makes life go pleasantly by for a season. In the race for coronets she often carries off the prize; but, once she has gained the victory, she is generous and forgives her English rivals everything, even their beauty.

Warned by the example of her mother that American women do not grow old gracefully, she tries not to grow old at all and often succeeds. She has exquisite feet and hands, and is always *bien chaussée et bien gantée* and can talk brilliantly upon any subject, provided that she knows nothing about it.

Her sense of humour keeps her from the tragedy of a *grande passion*, and, as there is neither romance nor humility in her love, she makes an excellent wife. What her ultimate influence on English life will be it is difficult to estimate at present; but there can be no doubt that, of all the factors that have contributed to the social revolution of London, there are few more important, and none more delightful, than the American Invasion.

Keats's 'Sonnet on Blue'

Century Guild Hobby Horse, July 1886

During my tour in America I happened one evening to find myself in Louisville, Kentucky. The subject I had selected to speak on was the Mission of Art in the Nineteenth Century, and in the course of my lecture I had occasion to quote Keats's 'Sonnet on Blue' as an example of the poet's delicate sense of colour-harmonies. When my lecture was concluded there came round to see me a lady of middle age, with a sweet gentle manner and a most musical voice. She introduced herself to me as Mrs Speed, the daughter of George Keats, and invited me to come and examine the Keats manuscripts in her possession. I spent most of the next day with her, reading the letters of Keats to her father, some of which were at that time unpublished, poring over torn yellow leaves and faded scraps of paper, and wondering at the little Dante in which Keats had written those marvellous notes on Milton. Some months afterwards, when I was in California, I received a letter from Mrs Speed asking my acceptance of the original manuscript of the sonnet which I had quoted in my lecture. This manuscript I have had reproduced here, as it seems to me to possess much psychological interest. It shows us the conditions that preceded the perfected form, the gradual growth, not of the conception but of the expression, and the workings of that spirit of selection which is the secret of style. In the case of poetry, as in the case of the other arts, what may appear to be simply technicalities of method are in their essence spiritual, not mechanical, and although, in all lovely work, what concerns us is the ultimate form, not the conditions that necessitate that form, yet the preference that precedes perfection, the evolution of the beauty, and the mere making of the music, have, if not their artistic value, at least their value to the artist.

It will be remembered that this sonnet was first published in 1848 by Lord Houghton in his *Life, Letters, and Literary Remains of John Keats*. Lord Houghton does not definitely state where he found it, but it was probably among the Keats manuscripts belonging to Mr Charles Brown. It is evidently taken from a version later than that in my possession, as it accepts all the corrections, and makes three variations. As in my manuscript the first line is torn away, I give the sonnet here as it appears in Lord Houghton's edition.

ANSWER TO A SONNET ENDING THUS:

Dark eyes are dearer far

Than those that make the hyacinthine bell.[1]

By J. H. Reynolds

Blue! 'Tis the life of heaven, – the domain
  Of Cynthia, – the wide palace of the sun, –
The tent of Hesperus and all his train, –
  The bosomer of clouds, gold, grey and dun.
Blue! 'Tis the life of waters – ocean
  And all its vassal streams: pools numberless
May rage, and foam, and fret, but never can
  Subside if not to dark-blue nativeness.
Blue! gentle cousin of the forest green,
  Married to green in all the sweetest flowers,
Forget-me-not, – the blue-bell, – and, that queen
  Of secrecy, the violet: what strange powers
Hast thou, as a mere shadow! But how great,
  When in an Eye thou art alive with fate!

February 1818

In the *Athenaeum* of the 3rd of June 1876, appeared a letter from Mr A. J. Horwood, stating that he had in his possession a copy of *The Garden of Florence* in which this sonnet was transcribed. Mr Horwood, who was unaware that the sonnet had been already published by Lord Houghton, gives the transcript at length. His

---

[1] 'Make' is of course a mere printer's error for 'mock,' and was subsequently corrected by Lord Houghton. The sonnet as given in *The Garden of Florence* reads 'orbs' for 'those.'

version reads *hue* for *life* in the first line, and *bright* for *wide* in the second, and gives the sixth line thus:

With all his tributary streams, pools numberless,

a foot too long: it also reads *to* for *of* in the ninth line. Mr Buxton Forman is of opinion that these variations are decidedly genuine, but indicative of an earlier state of the poem than that adopted in Lord Houghton's edition. However, now that we have before us Keats's first draft of his sonnet, it is difficult to believe that the sixth line in Mr Horwood's version is really a genuine variation. Keats may have written,

Ocean

His tributary streams, pools numberless,

and the transcript may have been carelessly made, but having got his line right in his first draft, Keats probably did not spoil it in his second. The *Athenaeum* version inserts a comma after *art* in the last line, which seems to me a decided improvement, and eminently characteristic of Keats's method. I am glad to see that Mr Buxton Forman has adopted it.

As for the corrections that Lord Houghton's version shows Keats to have made in the eighth and ninth lines of this sonnet, it is evident that they sprang from Keats's reluctance to repeat the same word in consecutive lines, except in cases where a word's music or meaning was to be emphasized. The substitution of 'its' for 'his' in the sixth line is more difficult of explanation. It was due probably to a desire on Keats's part not to mar by any echo the fine personification of Hesperus.

It may be noticed that Keats's own eyes were brown, and not blue, as stated by Mrs Proctor to Lord Houghton. Mrs Speed showed me a note to that effect written by Mrs George Keats on the margin of the page in Lord Houghton's *Life* (p. 100, vol. i.), where Mrs Proctor's description is given. Cowden Clarke made a similar correction in his *Recollections*, and in some of the later editions of Lord Houghton's book the word 'blue' is struck out. In Severn's portraits of Keats also the eyes are given as brown.

The exquisite sense of colour expressed in the ninth and tenth lines may be paralleled by

The Ocean with its vastness, its blue green,

of the sonnet to George Keats.

The Tomb of Keats

Irish Monthly, July 1877

As one enters Rome from the Via Ostiensis by the Porta San Paolo, the first object that meets the eye is a marble pyramid which stands close at hand on the left.

There are many Egyptian obelisks in Rome – tall, snakelike spires of red sandstone, mottled with strange writings, which remind us of the pillars of flame which led the children of Israel through the desert away from the land of the Pharaohs; but more wonderful than these to look upon is this gaunt, wedge-shaped pyramid standing here in this Italian city, unshattered amid the ruins and wrecks of time, looking older than the Eternal City itself, like terrible impassiveness turned to stone. And so in the Middle Ages men supposed this to be the sepulchre of Remus, who was slain by his own brother at the founding of the city, so ancient and mysterious it appears; but we have now, perhaps unfortunately, more accurate information about it, and know that it is the tomb of one Caius Cestius, a Roman gentleman of small note, who died about 30 BC.

Yet though we cannot care much for the dead man who lies in lonely state beneath it, and who is only known to the world through his sepulchre, still this pyramid will be ever dear to the eyes of all English-speaking people, because at evening its shadows fall on the tomb of one who walks with Spenser, and Shakespeare, and Byron, and Shelley, and Elizabeth Barrett Browning in the great procession of the sweet singers of England.

For at its foot there is a green, sunny slope, known as the Old Protestant Cemetery, and on this a common-looking grave, which bears the following inscription:

This grave contains all that was mortal of a young English poet, who

on his deathbed, in the bitterness of his heart, desired these words
to be engraven on his tombstone: HERE LIES ONE WHOSE NAME WAS
WRIT IN WATER. February 24, 1821.

And the name of the young English poet is John Keats.

Lord Houghton calls this cemetery 'one of the most beautiful
spots on which the eye and heart of man can rest', and Shelley
speaks of it as making one 'in love with death, to think that one
should be buried in so sweet a place'; and indeed when I saw
the violets and the daisies and the poppies that overgrow the
tomb, I remembered how the dead poet had once told his friend
that he thought the 'intensest pleasure he had received in life
was in watching the growth of flowers', and how another time,
after lying a while quite still, he murmured in some strange
prescience of early death, 'I feel the flowers growing over me'.

But this time-worn stone and these wild flowers are but poor
memorials[1] of one so great as Keats; most of all, too, in this city
of Rome, which pays such honour to her dead; where popes,
and emperors, and saints, and cardinals lie hidden in 'porphyry
wombs', or couched in baths of jasper and chalcedony and mala-
chite, ablaze with precious stones and metals, and tended with
continental service. For very noble is the site, and worthy of a
noble monument; behind looms the grey pyramid, symbol of the
world's age, and filled with memories of the sphinx, and the lotus
leaf, and the glories of old Nile: in front is the Monte Testaccio,
built, it is said, with the broken fragments of the vessels in which
all the nations of the East and the West brought their tribute to
Rome; and a little distance off, along the slope of the hill under

---

[1] Reverently some well-meaning persons have placed a marble slab on the wall
of the cemetery with a medallion-profile of Keats on it and some mediocre lines
of poetry. The face is ugly, and rather hatchet-shaped, with thick sensual lips,
and is utterly unlike the poet himself, who was very beautiful to look upon.
'His countenance,' says a lady who saw him at one of Hazlitt's lectures, 'lives
in my mind as one of singular beauty and brightness; it had the expression as
if he had been looking on some glorious sight.' And this is the idea which
Severn's picture of him gives. Even Haydon's rough pen-and-ink sketch of him
is better than this 'marble libel', which I hope will soon be taken down. I think
the best representation of the poet would be a coloured bust, like that of the
young Rajah of Koolapoor at Florence, which is a lovely and lifelike work of
art.

the Aurelian wall, some tall gaunt cypresses rise, like burnt-out funeral torches, to mark the spot where Shelley's heart (that 'heart of hearts'!) lies in the earth; and, above all, the soil on which we tread is very Rome!

As I stood beside the mean grave of this divine boy, I thought of him as of a Priest of Beauty slain before his time; and the vision of Guido's *St Sebastian* came before my eyes as I saw him at Genoa, a lovely brown boy, with crisp, clustering hair and red lips, bound by his evil enemies to a tree, and though pierced by arrows, raising his eyes with divine, impassioned gaze towards the Eternal Beauty of the opening heavens. And thus my thoughts shaped themselves to rhyme:

HEU MISERANDE PUER

Rid of the world's injustice and its pain,
   He rests at last beneath God's veil of blue;
   Taken from life while life and love were new
The youngest of the martyrs here is lain,
Fair as Sebastian and as foully slain.
   No cypress shades his grave, nor funeral yew,
   But red-lipped daisies, violets drenched with dew,
And sleepy poppies, catch the evening rain.

O proudest heart that broke for misery!
   O saddest poet that the world hath seen!
      O sweetest singer of the English land!
      Thy name was writ in water on the sand,
   But our tears shall keep thy memory green,
And make it flourish like a Basil-tree.

Rome, 1877

Note. A later version of this sonnet exists under the title of 'The Grave of Keats.'

Mr Whistler's Ten o'clock

Pall Mall Gazette, 21 February 1885

Last night, at Prince's Hall, Mr Whistler made his first public appearance as a lecturer on art, and spoke for more than an hour with really marvellous eloquence on the absolute uselessness of all lectures of the kind. Mr Whistler began his lecture with a very pretty *aria* on prehistoric history, describing how in earlier times hunter and warrior would go forth to chase and foray, while the artist sat at home making cup and bowl for their service. Rude imitations of nature they were first, like the gourd bottle, till the sense of beauty and form developed and, in all its exquisite proportions, the first vase was fashioned. Then came a higher civilization of architecture and armchairs, and with exquisite design, and dainty diaper, the useful things of life were made lovely; and the hunter and the warrior lay on the couch when they were tired, and, when they were thirsty, drank from the bowl, and never cared to lose the exquisite proportion of the one, or the delightful ornament of the other; and this attitude of the primitive anthropophagous Philistine formed the text of the lecture and was the attitude which Mr Whistler entreated his audience to adopt towards art. Remembering, no doubt, many charming invitations to wonderful private views, this fashionable assemblage seemed somewhat aghast, and not a little amused, at being told that the slightest appearance among a civilized people of any joy in beautiful things is a grave impertinence to all painters; but Mr Whistler was relentless, and, with charming ease and much grace of manner, explained to the public that the only thing they should cultivate was ugliness, and that on their permanent stupidity rested all the hopes of art in the future.

The scene was in every way delightful; he stood there, a miniature Mephistopheles, mocking the majority! He was like a brilliant surgeon lecturing to a class composed of subjects destined ultimately for dissection, and solemnly assuring them how valuable to science their maladies were, and how absolutely uninteresting the slightest symptoms of health on their part would be. In fairness to the audience, however, I must say that they seemed extremely gratified at being rid of the dreadful responsibility of admiring anything, and nothing could have exceeded their enthusiasm when they were told by Mr Whistler that no matter how vulgar their dresses were, or how hideous their surroundings at home, still it was possible that a great painter, if there was such a thing, could, by contemplating them in the twilight and half closing his eyes, see them under really picturesque conditions, and produce a picture which they were not to attempt to understand, much less dare to enjoy. Then there were some arrows, barbed and brilliant, shot off, with all the speed and splendour of fireworks, at the archaeologists, who spend their lives in verifying the birthplaces of nobodies, and estimate the value of a work of art by its date or its decay; at the art critics who always treat a picture as if it were a novel, and try and find out the plot; at dilettanti in general and amateurs in particular; and (*O mea culpa!*) at dress reformers most of all. 'Did not Velazquez paint crinolines? What more do you want?'

Having thus made a holocaust of humanity, Mr Whistler turned to nature, and in a few moments convicted her of the Crystal Palace, Bank holidays, and a general overcrowding of detail, both in omnibuses and in landscapes, and then, in a passage of singular beauty, not unlike one that occurs in Corot's letters, spoke of the artistic value of dim dawns and dusks, when the mean facts of life are lost in exquisite and evanescent effects, when common things are touched with mystery and transfigured with beauty, when the warehouses become as palaces and the tall chimneys of the factory seem like campaniles in the silver air.

Finally, after making a strong protest against anybody but a painter judging of painting, and a pathetic appeal to the audience not to be lured by the aesthetic movement into having beautiful things about them, Mr Whistler concluded his lecture with a pretty passage about Fusiyama on a fan, and made his bow to an audience which he had succeeded in completely fascinating by his wit, his brilliant paradoxes, and, at times, his real eloquence. Of course, with regard to the value of beautiful surroundings I differ entirely from Mr Whistler. An artist is not an isolated fact; he is the resultant of a certain *milieu* and a certain *entourage*, and can no more be born of a nation that is devoid of any sense of beauty than a fig can grow from a thorn or a rose blossom from a thistle. That an artist will find beauty in ugliness, *le beau dans l'horrible*, is now a commonplace of the schools, the *argot* of the atelier, but I strongly deny that charming people should be condemned to live with magenta ottomans and Albert-blue curtains in their rooms in order that some painter may observe the sidelights on the one and the values of the other. Nor do I accept the dictum that only a painter is a judge of painting. I say that only an artist is a judge of art: there is a wide difference. As long as a painter is a painter merely, he should not be allowed to talk of anything but mediums and megilp, and on those subjects should be compelled to hold his tongue; it is only when he becomes an artist that the secret laws of artistic creation are revealed to him. For there are not many arts, but one art merely – poem, picture and Parthenon, sonnet and statue – all are in their essence the same, and he who knows one knows all. But the poet is the supreme artist, for he is the master of colour and of form, and the real musician besides, and is lord over all life and all arts; and so to the poet beyond all others are these mysteries known; to Edgar Allan Poe and to Baudelaire, not to Benjamin West and Paul Delaroche. However, I should not enjoy anybody else's lectures unless in a few points I disagreed with them, and Mr Whistler's lecture last night was, like everything that he does, a masterpiece. Not merely for its clever satire and amusing jests will it be remembered, but for the pure and perfect beauty of many of its passages – passages delivered with an earnestness which seemed to amaze those who had looked on

Mr Whistler as a master of persiflage merely, and had not known him as we do, as a master of painting also. For that he is indeed one of the very greatest masters of painting is my opinion. And I may add that in this opinion Mr Whistler himself entirely concurs.

The Relation of Dress to Art

A note in Black and White on Mr Whistler's Lecture

Pall Mall Gazette, 28 February 1885

'How can you possibly paint these ugly three-cornered hats?' asked a reckless art critic once of Sir Joshua Reynolds. 'I see light and shade in them,' answered the artist. *'Les grands coloristes,'* says Baudelaire, in a charming article on the artistic value of frock coats, *'les grands coloristes savent faire de la couleur avec un habit noir, une cravate blanche, et un fond gris.'*

'Art seeks and finds the beautiful in all times, as did her high priest Rembrandt, when he saw the picturesque grandeur of the Jews' quarter of Amsterdam, and lamented not that its inhabitants were not Greeks,' were the fine and simple words used by Mr Whistler in one of the most valuable passages of his lecture. The most valuable, that is, to the painter: for there is nothing of which the ordinary English painter needs more to be reminded than that the true artist does not wait for life to be made picturesque for him, but sees life under picturesque conditions always – under conditions, that is to say, which are at once new and delightful. But between the attitude of the painter towards the public and the attitude of a people towards art, there is a wide difference. That, under certain conditions of light and shade, what is ugly in fact may in its effect become beautiful, is true; and this, indeed, is the real *modernité* of art: but these conditions are exactly what we cannot be always sure of, as we stroll down Piccadilly in the glaring vulgarity of the noonday, or lounge in the park with a foolish sunset as a background. Were we able to carry our *chiaroscuro* about with us, as we do our umbrellas, all would be well; but this being impossible, I hardly think that pretty and delightful people will continue to wear a style of dress as ugly as it is useless and as meaningless as it is monstrous, even on the chance of such a master as Mr Whistler spiritualizing them into a symphony or refining them into a mist. For the arts are made for life, and not life for the arts.

Nor do I feel quite sure that Mr Whistler has been himself always true to the dogma he seems to lay down, that a painter should paint only the dress of his age and of his actual surroundings: far be it from me to burden a butterfly with the heavy responsibility of its past: I have always been of the opinion that consistency is the last refuge of the unimaginative: but have we not all seen, and most of us admired, a picture from his hand of exquisite English girls strolling by an opal sea in the fantastic dresses of Japan? Has not Tite Street been thrilled with the tidings that the models of Chelsea were posing to the master, in peplums, for pastels?

Whatever comes from Mr Whistler's brush is far too perfect in its loveliness to stand or fall by any intellectual dogmas on art, even by his own: for Beauty is justified of all her children, and cares nothing for explanations; but it is impossible to look through any collection of modern pictures in London, from Burlington House to the Grosvenor Gallery, without feeling that the professional model is ruining painting and reducing it to a condition of mere pose and *pastiche*.

Are we not all weary of him, that venerable impostor fresh from the steps of the Piazza di Spagna, who, in the leisure moments that he can spare from his customary organ, makes the round of the studios and is waited for in Holland Park? Do we not all recognize him, when, with the gay *insouciance* of his nation, he reappears on the walls of our summer exhibitions as everything that he is not, and as nothing that he is, glaring at us here as a patriarch of Canaan, here beaming as a brigand from the Abruzzi? Popular is he, this poor peripatetic professor of posing, with those whose joy it is to paint the posthumous portrait of the last philanthropist who in his lifetime had neglected to be photographed – yet he is the sign of the decadence, the symbol of decay.

For all costumes are caricatures. The basis of Art is not the Fancy Ball. Where there is loveliness of dress, there is no dressing up. And so, were our national attire delightful in colour, and in construction simple and sincere; were dress the expression of the loveliness that it shields and of the swiftness and motion that it does not impede; did its lines break from the shoulder instead of bulging from the waist; did the inverted wineglass cease to be the ideal of form; were these things brought about, as brought about they will be, then would painting be no longer an artificial reaction against the ugliness of life, but become, as it should be, the natural expression of life's beauty. Nor would painting merely, but all the other arts also, be the gainers by a change such as that which I propose; the gainers, I mean, through the increased atmosphere of Beauty by which the artists would be surrounded and in which they would grow up. For Art is not to be taught in Academies. It is what one looks at, not what one listens to, that makes the artist. The real schools should be the streets. There is not, for instance, a single delicate line, or delightful proportion, in the dress of the Greeks, which is not echoed exquisitely in their architecture. A nation arrayed in stove-pipe hats and dress-improvers might have built the Pantechnicon possibly, but the Parthenon never. And finally, there is this to be said: art, it is true, can never have any other claim but her own perfection, and it may be that the artist, desiring merely to contemplate and to create, is wise in not busying himself about change in others: yet wisdom is not always the best; there are times when she sinks to the level of common sense; and from the passionate folly of those – and there are many – who desire that Beauty shall be confined no longer to the *bric-à-brac* of the collector and the dust of the museum, but shall be, as it should be, the natural and national inheritance of all – from this noble unwisdom, I say, who knows what new loveliness shall be given to life, and, under these more exquisite conditions, what perfect artist born? *Le milieu se renouvelant, l'art se renouvelle.*

Speaking, however, from his own passionless pedestal, Mr Whistler, in pointing out that the power of the painter is to be found in his power of vision, not in his cleverness of hand, has expressed a truth which needed expression, and which, coming from the lord of form and colour, cannot fail to have its influence. His lecture, the Apocrypha though it be for the people, yet remains from this time as the Bible for the painter, the masterpiece of masterpieces, the song of songs. It is true he has pronounced the panegyric of the Philistine, but I fancy Ariel praising Caliban for a jest: and, in that he has read the Commination Service over the critics, let all men thank him, the critics themselves, indeed, most of all, for he has now relieved them from the necessity of a tedious existence. Considered, again, merely as an orator, Mr Whistler seems to me to stand almost alone. Indeed, among all our public speakers I know but few who can combine so felicitously as he does the mirth and malice of Puck with the style of the minor prophets.

Woman's Dress

Pall Mall Gazette, 14 October 1884

Mr Oscar Wilde, who asks us to permit him 'that most charming of all pleasures, the pleasure of answering one's critics', sends us the following remarks:

The 'Girl Graduate' must of course have precedence, not merely for her sex but for her sanity: her letter is extremely sensible. She makes two points: that high heels are a necessity for any lady who wishes to keep her dress clean from the Stygian mud of our streets, and that without a tight corset 'the ordinary number of petticoats and etceteras' cannot be properly or conveniently held up. Now, it is quite true that as long as the lower garments are suspended from the hips a corset is an absolute necessity; the mistake lies in not suspending all apparel from the shoulder. In the latter case a corset becomes useless, the body is left free and unconfined for respiration and motion, there is more health, and consequently more beauty. Indeed all the most ungainly and uncomfortable articles of dress that fashion has ever in her folly prescribed, not the tight corset merely, but the farthingale, the vertugadin, the hoop, the crinoline, and that modern monstrosity the so-called 'dress-improver' also, all of them have owed their origin to the same error, the error of not seeing that it is from the shoulders, and from the shoulders only, that all garments should be hung.

And as regards high heels, I quite admit that some additional height to the shoe or boot is necessary if long gowns are to be worn in the street; but what I object to is that the height should be given to the heel only, and not to the sole of the foot also. The modern high-heeled boot is, in fact, merely the clog of the time of Henry VI, with the front prop left out, and its most inevitable effect is to throw the body forward, to shorten the steps, and consequently to produce that want of grace which always follows want of freedom.

Why should clogs be despised? Much art has been expended on clogs. They have been made of lovely woods, and delicately inlaid with ivory, and with mother-of-pearl. A clog might be a dream of beauty, and if not too high or too heavy, most comfortable also. But if there be any who do not like clogs, let them try some adaptation of the trousers of the Turkish lady, which is loose round the limb and tight at the ankle.

The 'Girl Graduate', with a pathos to which I am not insensible, entreats me not to apotheosize 'that awful, befringed, beflounced and bekilted divided skirt'. Well, I will acknowledge that the fringes, the flounces and the kilting do certainly defeat the whole object of the dress, which is that of ease and liberty; but I regard these things as mere superfluities, tragic proofs that the divided skirt is ashamed of its own division. The principle of the dress is good, and though it is not by any means perfection, it is a step towards it.

Here I leave the 'Girl Graduate', with much regret, for Mr Wentworth Huyshe. Mr Huyshe makes the old criticism that Greek dress is unsuited to our climate, and, to me the somewhat new assertion, that the men's dress of a hundred years ago was preferable to that of the second part of the seventeenth century, which I consider to have been the exquisite period of English costume. Now, as regards the first of these two statements, I will say, to begin with, that the warmth of apparel does not depend really on the number of garments worn, but on the material of which they are made. One of the chief faults of modern dress is that it is composed of far too many articles of clothing, most of which are of the wrong substance; but over a substratum of pure wool, such as supplied by Dr Jaeger under the modern German system, some modification of the Greek costume is perfectly applicable to our climate, our country and our century. This important fact has already been pointed out by Mr E. W. Godwin in his excellent, though too brief, handbook on *Dress*, contributed to the Health Exhibition. I call it an important fact because it makes almost any form of lovely costume perfectly practicable in our cold climate. Mr Godwin, it is true, points out that the English ladies of the thirteenth century abandoned after some time the flowing garments of the early Renaissance in favour of a tighter mode, such as Northern Europe seems to demand. This I quite admit, and its significance; but what I contend, and what I am sure Mr Godwin would agree with me in, is that the principles, the laws of Greek dress may be perfectly realized, even in a moderately tight gown with sleeves: I mean the principle of suspending all apparel from the shoulders, and of relying for beauty of effect not on the stiff ready-made ornaments of the modern milliner – the bows where there should be no bows, and the flounces where there should be no flounces – but on the exquisite play of light and line that one gets from rich and rippling folds. I am not proposing an antiquarian revival of an ancient costume, but trying merely to point out the right laws of dress, laws which are dictated by art and not by archaeology, by science and not by fashion; and just as the best work of art in our days is that which combines classic grace with absolute reality, so from a continuation of the Greek principles of beauty with the German principles of health will come, I feel certain, the costume of the future.

And now to the question of men's dress, or rather to Mr Huyshe's claim of the superiority, in point of costume, of the last quarter of the eighteenth century over the second quarter of the seventeenth. The broad-brimmed hat of 1640 kept the rain of winter and the glare of summer from the face; the same cannot be said of the hat of one hundred years ago, which, with its comparatively narrow brim and high crown, was the precursor of the modern 'chimney-pot': a wide turned-down collar is a healthier thing than a strangling stock, and a short cloak much more comfortable than a sleeved overcoat, even though the latter may have had 'three capes'; a cloak is easier to put on and off, lies lightly on the shoulders in summer, and wrapped round one in winter keeps one perfectly warm. A doublet, again, is simpler than a coat and waistcoat; instead of two garments one has one; by not being open it also protects the chest better.

Short loose trousers are in every way to be preferred to the tight knee-breeches which often impede the proper circulation of the blood; and finally, the soft leather boots which could be worn above or below the knee, are more supple, and give consequently more freedom, than the stiff Hessian which Mr Huyshe so praises. I say nothing about the question of grace and picturesqueness, for I suppose that no one, not even Mr Huyshe, would prefer a maccaroni to a cavalier, a Lawrence to a Vandyke, or the third George to the first Charles; but for ease, warmth and comfort this seventeenth-century dress is infinitely superior to anything that came after it, and I do not think it is excelled by any preceding form of costume. I sincerely trust that we may soon see in England some national revival of it.

English Poetesses

Queen, 8 December 1888

England has given to the world one great poetess, Elizabeth Barrett Browning. By her side Mr Swinburne would place Miss Christina Rossetti, whose New Year hymn he describes as so much the noblest of sacred poems in our language, that there is none which comes near it enough to stand second. 'It is a hymn,' he tells us, 'touched as with the fire, and bathed as in the light of sunbeams, tuned as to chords and cadences of refluent sea-music beyond reach of harp and organ, large echoes of the serene and sonorous tides of heaven.' Much as I admire Miss Rossetti's work, her subtle choice of words, her rich imagery, her artistic *naïveté*, wherein curious notes of strangeness and simplicity are fantastically blended together, I cannot but think that Mr Swinburne has, with noble and natural loyalty, placed her on too lofty a pedestal. To me, she is simply a very delightful artist in poetry. This is indeed something so rare that when we meet it we cannot fail to love it, but it is not everything. Beyond it and above it are higher and more sunlit heights of song, a larger vision, and an ampler air, a music at once more passionate and more profound, a creative energy that is born of the spirit, a winged rapture that is born of the soul, a force and fervour of mere utterance that has all the wonder of the prophet, and not a little of the consecration of the priest.

Mrs Browning is unapproachable by any woman who has ever touched lyre or blown through reed since the days of the great Aeolian poetess. But Sappho, who, to the antique world was a pillar of flame, is to us but a pillar of shadow. Of her poems, burnt with other most precious work by Byzantine Emperor and by Roman Pope, only a few fragments remain. Possibly they lie mouldering in the scented darkness of an Egyptian tomb, clasped in the withered hands of some long-dead lover. Some Greek monk at Athos may even now be poring over an ancient manuscript, whose crabbed characters conceal lyric or ode by her whom the Greeks spoke of as 'the Poetess' just as they termed Homer 'the Poet', who was to them the tenth Muse, the flower of the Graces, the child of Eros, and the pride of Hellas – Sappho, with the sweet voice, the bright, beautiful eyes, the dark hyacinth-coloured hair. But, practically, the work of the marvellous singer of Lesbos is entirely lost to us.

We have a few rose leaves out of her garden, that is all. Literature nowadays survives marble and bronze, but in old days, in spite of the Roman poet's noble boast, it was not so. The fragile clay vases of the Greeks still keep for us pictures of Sappho, delicately painted in black and red and white; but of her song we have only the echo of an echo.

Of all the women of history, Mrs Browning is the only one that we could name in any possible or remote conjunction with Sappho.

Sappho was undoubtedly a far more flawless and perfect artist. She stirred the whole antique world more than Mrs Browning ever stirred our modern age. Never had Love such a singer. Even in the few lines that remain to us the passion seems to scorch and burn. But, as unjust Time, who has crowned her with the barren laurels of fame, has twined with them the dull poppies of oblivion, let us turn from the mere memory of a poetess to one whose song still remains to us as an imperishable glory to our literature; to her who heard the cry of the children from dark mine and crowded factory, and made England weep over its little ones; who, in the feigned sonnets from the Portuguese, sang of the spiritual mystery of Love, and of the intellectual gifts that Love brings to the soul; who had faith in all that is worthy, and enthusiasm for all that is great, and pity for all that suffers: who wrote the *Vision of Poets* and *Casa Guidi Windows* and *Aurora Leigh*.

As one, to whom I owe my love of poetry no less than my love of country, has said of her:

> Still on our ears
> The clear 'Excelsior' from a woman's lip

Rings out across the Apennines, although
The woman's brow lies pale and cold in death
With all the mighty marble dead in Florence.
For while great songs can stir the hearts of men,
Spreading their full vibrations through the world
In ever-widening circles till they reach
The Throne of God, and song becomes a prayer,
And prayer brings down the liberating strength
That kindles nations to heroic deeds,
She lives – the great-souled poetess who saw
From Casa Guidi windows Freedom dawn
On Italy, and gave the glory back
In sunrise hymns to all Humanity!

She lives indeed, and not alone in the heart of Shakespeare's England, but in the heart of Dante's Italy also. To Greek literature she owed her scholarly culture, but modern Italy created her human passion for Liberty. When she crossed the Alps she became filled with a new ardour, and from that fine, eloquent mouth, that we can still see in her portraits, broke forth such a noble and majestic outburst of lyrical song as had not been heard from woman's lips for more than two thousand years. It is pleasant to think that an English poetess was to a certain extent a real factor in bringing about that unity of Italy that was Dante's dream, and if Florence drove her great singer into exile, she at least welcomed within her walls the later singer that England had sent to her.

If one were asked the chief qualities of Mrs Browning's work, one would say, as Mr Swinburne said of Byron's, its sincerity and its strength. Faults it, of course, possesses. 'She would rhyme moon to table,' used to be said of her in jest; and certainly no more monstrous rhymes are to be found in all literature than some of those we come across in Mrs Browning's poems. But her ruggedness was never the result of carelessness. It was deliberate, as her letters to Mr Horne show very clearly. She refused to sandpaper her muse. She disliked facile smoothness and artificial polish. In her very rejection of art she was an artist. She intended to produce a certain effect by certain means, and she succeeded; and her indifference to complete assonance in rhyme often gives a splendid richness to her verse, and brings into it a pleasurable element of surprise.

In philosophy she was a Platonist, in politics an Opportunist. She attached herself to no particular party. She loved the people when they were king-like, and kings when they showed themselves to be men. Of the real value and motive of poetry she had a most exalted idea. 'Poetry,' she says, in the preface of one of her volumes, 'has been as serious a thing to me as life itself; and life has been a very serious thing. There has been no playing at skittles for me in either. I never mistook pleasure for the final cause of poetry, nor leisure for the hour of the poet. I have done my work so far, not as mere hand and head work apart from the personal being, but as the completest expression of that being to which I could attain.'

It certainly is her completest expression, and through it she realizes her fullest perfection. 'The poet,' she says elsewhere, 'is at once richer and poorer than he used to be; he wears better broadcloth, but speaks no more oracles.' These words give us the keynote to her view of the poet's mission. He was to utter Divine oracles, to be at once inspired prophet and holy priest; and as such we may, I think, without exaggeration, conceive her. She was a Sibyl delivering a message to the world, sometimes through stammering lips, and once at least with blinded eyes, yet always with the true fire and fervour of lofty and unshaken faith, always with the great raptures of a spiritual nature, the high ardours of an impassioned soul. As we read her best poems we feel that, though Apollo's shrine be empty and the bronze tripod overthrown, and the vale of Delphi desolate, still the Pythia is not dead. In our own age she has sung for us, and this land gave her new birth. Indeed, Mrs Browning is the wisest of the Sibyls, wiser even than that mighty figure whom Michelangelo has painted on the roof of the Sistine Chapel at Rome, poring over the scroll of mystery, and trying to decipher the secrets of Fate; for she realized that, while knowledge is power, suffering is part of knowledge.

To her influence, almost as much as to the higher education of women, I would be inclined to attribute the really remarkable awakening of woman's song that characterizes the latter half of

our century in England. No country has ever had so many
poetesses at once. Indeed, when one remembers that the Greeks
had only nine muses, one is sometimes apt to fancy that we have
too many. And yet the work done by women in the sphere of
poetry is really of a very high standard of excellence. In England
we have always been prone to underrate the value of tradition
in literature. In our eagerness to find a new voice and a fresh
mode of music, we have forgotten how beautiful Echo may be.
We look first for individuality and personality, and these are,
indeed, the chief characteristics of the masterpieces of our literature, either in prose or verse; but deliberate culture and a study
of the best models, if united to an artistic temperament and a
nature susceptible of exquisite impressions, may produce much
that is admirable, much that is worthy of praise. It would be
quite impossible to give a complete catalogue of all the women
who since Mrs Browning's day have tried lute and lyre. Mrs
Pfeiffer, Mrs Hamilton King, Mrs Augusta Webster, Graham
Tomson, Miss Mary Robinson, Jean Ingelow, Miss May Kend-
all, Miss Nesbit, Miss May Probyn, Mrs Craik, Mrs Meynell,
Miss Chapman and many others have done really good work
in poetry, either in the grave Dorian mode of thoughtful and
intellectual verse, or in the light and graceful forms of old French
song, or in the romantic manner of antique ballad, or in that
'moment's monument', as Rossetti called it, the intense and
concentrated sonnet. Occasionally one is tempted to wish that the
quick artistic faculty that women undoubtedly possess developed
itself somewhat more in prose and somewhat less in verse. Poetry
is for our highest moods, when we wish to be with the gods, and
in our poetry nothing but the very best should satisfy us; but
prose is for our daily bread, and the lack of good prose is one of
the chief blots on our culture. French prose, even in the hands
of the most ordinary writers, is always readable, but English
prose is detestable. We have a few, a very few, masters, such as
they are. We have Carlyle, who should not be imitated; and Mr
Pater, who, through the subtle perfection of his form, is inimitable absolutely; and Mr Froude, who is useful; and Matthew
Arnold, who is a model; and Mr George Meredith, who is a
warning; and Mr Lang, who is the divine amateur; and Mr

Stevenson, who is the humane artist; and Mr Ruskin, whose rhythm and colour and fine rhetoric and marvellous music of words are entirely unattainable. But the general prose that one reads in magazines and in newspapers is terribly dull and cumbrous, heavy in movement and uncouth or exaggerated in expression. Possibly some day our women of letters will apply themselves more definitely to prose.

Their light touch and exquisite ear, and delicate sense of balance and proportion, would be of no small service to us. I can fancy women bringing a new manner into our literature.

However, we have to deal here with women as poetesses, and it is interesting to note that, though Mrs Browning's influence undoubtedly contributed very largely to the development of this new song-movement, if I may so term it, still there seems to have been never a time during the last three hundred years when the women of this kingdom did not cultivate, if not the art, at least the habit, of writing poetry.

Who the first English poetess was I cannot say. I believe it was the Abbess Juliana Berners, who lived in the fifteenth century; but I have no doubt that Mr Freeman would be able at a moment's notice to produce some wonderful Saxon or Norman poetess, whose works cannot be read without a glossary, and even with its aid are completely unintelligible. For my own part, I am content with the Abbess Juliana, who wrote enthusiastically about hawking; and after her I would mention Anne Askew, who in prison and on the eve of her fiery martyrdom wrote a ballad that has, at any rate, a pathetic and historical interest. Queen Elizabeth's 'most sweet and sententious ditty' on Mary Stuart is highly praised by Puttenham, a contemporary critic, as an example of 'Exargasia, or the Gorgeous in Literature', which somehow seems a very suitable epithet for such a great Queen's poems. The term she applies to the unfortunate Queen of Scots, 'the daughter of debate', has, of course, long since passed into literature. The Countess of Pembroke, Sir Philip Sidney's sister, was much admired as a poetess in her day.

In 1613 the 'learned, virtuous, and truly noble ladie', Elizabeth Carew, published a *Tragedie of Marian, the Faire Queene of Jewry*, and a few years later the 'noble ladie Diana Primrose' wrote *A*

Chain of Pearl, which is a panegyric on the 'peerless graces' of Gloriana. Mary Morpeth, the friend and admirer of Drummond of Hawthornden; Lady Mary Wroth, to whom Ben Jonson dedicated *The Alchemist*; and the Princess Elizabeth, the sister of Charles I, should also be mentioned.

After the Restoration women applied themselves with still greater ardour to the study of literature and the practice of poetry. Margaret, Duchess of Newcastle, was a true woman of letters, and some of her verses are extremely pretty and graceful. Mrs Aphra Behn was the first Englishwoman who adopted literature as a regular profession. Mrs Katharine Philips, according to Mr Gosse, invented sentimentality. As she was praised by Dryden, and mourned by Cowley, let us hope she may be forgiven. Keats came across her poems at Oxford when he was writing *Endymion*, and found in one of them 'a most delicate fancy of the Fletcher kind'; but I fear nobody reads the Matchless Orinda now. Of Lady Winchelsea's *Nocturnal Reverie* Wordsworth said that, with the exception of Pope's *Windsor Forest*, it was the only poem of the period intervening between *Paradise Lost* and Thomson's *Seasons* that contained a single new image of external nature. Lady Rachel Russell, who may be said to have inaugurated the letter-writing literature of England; Eliza Haywood, who is immortalized by the badness of her work, and has a niche in *The Dunciad*; and the Marchioness of Wharton, whose poems Waller said he admired, are very remarkable types, the finest of them being, of course, the first named, who was a woman of heroic mould and of a most noble dignity of nature.

Indeed, though the English poetesses up to the time of Mrs Browning cannot be said to have produced any work of absolute genius, they are certainly interesting figures, fascinating subjects for study. Amongst them we find Lady Mary Wortley Montague, who had all the caprice of Cleopatra, and whose letters are delightful reading; Mrs Centlivre, who wrote one brilliant comedy; Lady Anne Barnard, whose *Auld Robin Gray* was described by Sir Walter Scott as 'worth all the dialogues Corydon and Phillis have together spoken from the days of Theocritus downwards', and is certainly a very beautiful and touching poem; Esther Vanhomrigh and Hester Johnson, the Vanessa and the

Stella of Dean Swift's life; Mrs Thrale, the friend of the great lexicographer; the worthy Mrs Barbauld; the excellent Mrs Hannah More; the industrious Joanna Baillie; the admirable Mrs Chapone, whose *Ode to Solitude* always fills me with the wildest passion for society, and who will at least be remembered as the patroness of the establishment at which Becky Sharp was educated; Miss Anna Seward, who was called 'The Swan of Lichfield'; poor L. E. L., whom Disraeli described in one of his clever letters to his sister as 'the personification of Brompton – pink satin dress, white satin shoes, red cheeks, snub nose, and her hair *à la* Sappho'; Mrs Ratcliffe, who introduced the romantic novel, and has consequently much to answer for; the beautiful Duchess of Devonshire, of whom Gibbon said that she was 'made for something better than a Duchess'; the two wonderful sisters, Lady Dufferin and Mrs Norton; Mrs Tighe, whose *Psyche* Keats read with pleasure; Constantia Grierson, a marvellous blue-stocking in her time: Mrs Hemans; pretty, charming 'Perdita', who flirted alternately with poetry and the Prince Regent, played divinely in the *Winter's Tale*, was brutally attacked by Gifford, and has left us a pathetic little poem on the Snowdrop; and Emily Brontë, whose poems are instinct with tragic power, and seem often on the verge of being great.

Old fashions in literature are not so pleasant as old fashions in dress. I like the costume of the age of powder better than the poetry of the age of Pope. But if one adopts the historical stand-point – and this is, indeed, the only standpoint from which we can ever form a fair estimate of work that is not absolutely of the highest order – we cannot fail to see that many of the English poetesses who preceded Mrs Browning were women of no ordinary talent, and that if the majority of them looked upon poetry simply as a department of *belles lettres*, so in most cases did their contemporaries. Since Mrs Browning's day our woods have become full of singing birds, and if I venture to ask them to apply themselves more to prose and less to song, it is not that I like poetical prose, but that I love the prose of poets.

Mrs Langtry
as Hester Grazebrook

New York World, 7 November 1882

It is only in the best Greek gems, on the silver coins of Syracuse, or among the marble figures of the Parthenon frieze, that one can find the ideal representation of the marvellous beauty of that face which laughed through the leaves last night as Hester Grazebrook.

Pure Greek it is, with the grave low forehead, the exquisitely arched brow; the noble chiselling of the mouth, shaped as if it were the mouthpiece of an instrument of music; the supreme and splendid curve of the cheek; the augustly pillared throat which bears it all: it is Greek, because the lines which compose it are so definite and so strong, and yet so exquisitely harmonized that the effect is one of simple loveliness purely: Greek, because its essence and its quality, as is the quality of music and of architecture, is that of beauty based on absolutely mathematical laws.

But while art remains dumb and immobile in its passionless serenity, with the beauty of this face it is different: the grey eyes lighten into blue or deepen into violet as fancy succeeds fancy; the lips become flower-like in laughter or, tremulous as a bird's wing, mould themselves at last into the strong and bitter moulds of pain or scorn. And then motion comes, and the statue wakes into life. But the life is not the ordinary life of common days; it is life with a new value given to it, the value of art: and the charm to me of Hester Grazebrook's acting in the first scene of the play[1] last night was that mingling of classic grace with absolute reality which is the secret of all beautiful art, of the

---

[1] *An Unequal Match*, by Tom Taylor, at Wallack's Theatre, New York, 6 November 1882.

plastic work of the Greeks and of the pictures of Jean François Millet equally.

I do not think that the sovereignty and empire of women's beauty has at all passed away, though we may no longer go to war for them as the Greeks did for the daughter of Leda. The greatest empire still remains for them – the empire of art. And, indeed, this wonderful face, seen last night for the first time in America, has filled and permeated with the pervading image of its type the whole of our modern art in England. Last century it was the romantic type which dominated in art, the type loved by Reynolds and Gainsborough, of wonderful contrasts of colour, of exquisite and varying charm of expression, but without that definite plastic feeling which divides classic from romantic work. This type degenerated into mere facile prettiness in the hands of lesser masters, and, in protest against it, was created by the hands of the Pre-Raphaelites a new type, with its rare combination of Greek form with Florentine mysticism. But this mysticism becomes overstrained and a burden, rather than an aid to expression, and a desire for the pure Hellenic joy and serenity came in its place; and in all our modern work, in the paintings of such men as Albert Moore and Leighton and Whistler, we can trace the influence of this single face giving fresh life and inspiration in the form of a new artistic ideal.

As regards Hester Grazebrook's dresses, the first was a dress whose grace depended entirely on the grace of the person who wore it. It was merely the simple dress of a village girl in England. The second was a lovely combination of blue and creamy lace. But the masterpiece was undoubtedly the last, a symphony in silver-grey and pink, a pure melody of colour which I feel sure Whistler would call a *Scherzo*, and take as its visible motive the moonlight wandering in silver mist through a rose garden; unless indeed he saw this dress, in which case he would paint it and nothing else, for it is a dress such as Velazquez only could paint, and Whistler very wisely always paints those things which are within reach of Velazquez only.

The scenery was, of course, prepared in a hurry. Still, much of it was very good indeed: the first scene especially, with its graceful trees and open forge and cottage porch, though the roses were dreadfully out of tone and, besides their crudity of colour, were curiously badly grouped. The last scene was exceedingly clever and true to nature as well, being that combination of lovely scenery and execrable architecture which is so specially characteristic of a German spa. As for the drawing-room scene, I cannot regard it as in any way a success. The heavy ebony doors are entirely out of keeping with the satin panels; the silk hangings and festoons of black and yellow are quite meaningless in their position and consequently quite ugly; the carpet is out of all colour relation with the rest of the room, and the table-cover is mauve. Still, to have decorated even so bad a room in six days must, I suppose, be a subject of respectful wonder, though I should have fancied that Mr Wallack had many very much better sets in his own stock.

But I am beginning to quarrel generally with most modern scene-painting. A scene is primarily a decorative background for the actors, and should always be kept subordinate, first to the players, their dress, gesture and action; and secondly, to the fundamental principle of decorative art, which is not to imitate but to suggest nature. If the landscape is given its full realistic value, the value of the figures to which it serves as a background is impaired and often lost, and so the painted hangings of the Elizabethan age were a far more artistic, and so a far more rational form of scenery than most modern scene-painting is. From the same master-hand which designed the curtain of Madison Square Theatre I should like very much to see a good decorative landscape in scene-painting; for I have seen no open-air scene in any theatre which did not really mar the value of the actors. One must either, like Titian, make the landscape subordinate to the figures, or, like Claude, the figures subordinate to the landscape; for if we desire realistic acting we cannot have realistic scene-painting.

I need not describe, however, how the beauty of Hester Grazebrook survived the crude roses and the mauve tablecloth triumphantly. That it is a beauty that will be appreciated to the full in America I do not doubt for a moment, for it is only countries which possess great beauty that can appreciate beauty at all. It may also influence the art of America as it has influenced the art of England, for of the rare Greek type it is the most absolutely perfect example.

The Philistine may, of course, object that to be absolutely perfect is impossible. Well, that is so: but then it is only the impossible things that are worth doing nowadays!

Shakespeare on Scenery

Dramatic Review, 14 March 1885

I have often heard people wonder what Shakespeare would say, could he see Mr Irving's production of his *Much Ado About Nothing*, or Mr Wilson Barrett's setting of his *Hamlet*. Would he take pleasure in the glory of the scenery and the marvel of the colour? Would he be interested in the Cathedral of Messina, and the battlements of Elsinore? Or would he be indifferent, and say the play, and the play only, is the thing?

Speculations like these are always pleasurable, and in the present case happen to be profitable also. For it is not difficult to see what Shakespeare's attitude would be; not difficult, that is to say, if one reads Shakespeare himself, instead of reading merely what is written about him.

Speaking, for instance, directly, as the manager of a London theatre, through the lips of the chorus in *Henry V*, he complains of the smallness of the stage on which he has to produce the pageant of a big historical play, and of the want of scenery which obliges him to cut out many of its most picturesque incidents, apologizes for the scanty number of supers who had to play the soldiers, and for the shabbiness of the properties, and, finally, expresses his regret at being unable to bring on real horses.

In the *Midsummer Night's Dream*, again, he gives us a most amusing picture of the straits to which theatrical managers of his day were reduced by the want of proper scenery. In fact, it is impossible to read him without seeing that he is constantly protesting against the two special limitations of the Elizabethan stage – the lack of suitable scenery, and the fashion of men playing women's parts, just as he protests against other difficulties with which managers of theatres have still to contend, such as actors who do not understand their words; actors who miss their cues; actors who overact their parts; actors who mouth; actors who gag; actors who play to the gallery, and amateur actors.

And, indeed, a great dramatist, as he was, could not but have felt very much hampered at being obliged continually to interrupt the progress of a play in order to send on someone to explain to the audience that the scene was to be changed to a particular place on the entrance of a particular character, and after his exit to somewhere else; that the stage was to represent the deck of a ship in a storm, or the interior of a Greek temple, or the streets of a certain town, to all of which inartistic devices Shakespeare is reduced, and for which he always amply apologizes. Besides this clumsy method, Shakespeare had two other substitutes for scenery – the hanging out of a placard, and his descriptions. The first of these could hardly have satisfied his passion for picturesqueness and his feeling for beauty, and certainly did not satisfy the dramatic critic of his day. But as regards the description, to those of us who look on Shakespeare not merely as a playwright but as a poet, and who enjoy reading him at home just as much as we enjoy seeing him acted, it may be a matter of congratulation that he had not at his command such skilled machinists as are in use now at the Princess's and at the Lyceum. For had Cleopatra's barge, for instance, been a structure of canvas and Dutch metal, it would probably have been painted over or broken up after the withdrawal of the piece, and, even had it survived to our own day, would, I am afraid, have become extremely shabby by this time. Whereas now the beaten gold of its poop is still bright, and the purple of its sails still beautiful; its silver oars are not tired of keeping time to the music of the flutes they follow, nor the Nereid's flower-soft hands of touching its silken tackle; the mermaid still lies at its helm, and still on its deck stand the boys with their coloured fans. Yet lovely as all Shakespeare's descriptive passages are, a description is in its essence undramatic. Theatrical audiences are far more impressed by what they look at than by what they listen to; and the modern dramatist, in having the surroundings of his play visibly presented to the audience when the curtain rises, enjoys an advantage for which Shakespeare often expresses his desire. It is true that Shakespeare's descriptions are not what descriptions are in modern plays – accounts of what the audience can observe for themselves; they are the imaginative method by which he creates in the mind of the spectators the image of that which he desires them to see. Still, the quality of the drama is action. It is always dangerous to pause for picturesqueness. And the introduction of self-explanatory scenery enables the modern method to be far more direct, while the loveliness of form and colour which it gives us, seems to me often to create an artistic temperament in the audience, and to produce that joy in beauty for beauty's sake, without which the great masterpieces of art can never be understood, to which, and to which only, are they ever revealed.

To talk of the passion of a play being hidden by the paint, and of sentiment being killed by scenery, is mere emptiness and folly of words. A noble play, nobly mounted, gives us double artistic pleasure. The eye as well as the ear is gratified, and the whole nature is made exquisitely receptive of the influence of imaginative work. And as regards a bad play, have we not all seen large audiences lured by the loveliness of scenic effect into listening to rhetoric posing as poetry, and to vulgarity doing duty for realism? Whether this be good or evil for the public I will not here discuss, but it is evident that the playwright, at any rate, never suffers.

Indeed, the artist who really has suffered through the modern mounting of plays is not the dramatist at all, but the scene-painter proper. He is rapidly being displaced by the stage carpenter. Now and then, at Drury Lane, I have seen beautiful old front cloths let down, as perfect as pictures some of them, and pure painter's work, and there are many which we all remember at other theatres, in front of which some dialogue was reduced to graceful dumb show through the hammer and tin-tacks behind. But as a rule the stage is overcrowded with enormous properties, which are not merely far more expensive and cumbersome than scene-paintings, but far less beautiful, and far less true. Properties kill perspective. A painted door is more like a real door than a real door is itself, for the proper conditions of light and shade can be given to it; and the excessive use of built up structures always makes the stage too glaring, for as they have to be lit from behind, as well as from the front, the gas-jets become the absolute light of the scene instead of the means merely by which we perceive the conditions of light and shadow which the painter has desired to show us.

So, instead of bemoaning the position of the playwright, it were better for the critics to exert whatever influence they may possess towards restoring the scene-painter to his proper position as an artist, and not allowing him to be built over by the property man, or hammered to death by the carpenter. I have never seen any reason myself why such artists as Mr Beverley, Mr Walter Hann and Mr Telbin should not be entitled to become Academicians. They have certainly as good a claim as have many of those RAs whose total inability to paint we can see every May for a shilling.

And lastly, let those critics who hold up for our admiration the simplicity of the Elizabethan Stage, remember that they are lauding a condition of things against which Shakespeare himself, in the spirit of a true artist, always strongly protested.

Hamlet *at the Lyceum*

Dramatic Review, 9 May 1885

It sometimes happens that at a *première* in London the least enjoyable part of the performance is the play. I have seen many audiences more interesting than the actors, and have often heard better dialogue in the *foyer* than I have on the stage. At the Lyceum, however, this is rarely the case, and when the play is a play of Shakespeare's, and among its exponents are Mr Irving and Miss Ellen Terry, we turn from the gods in the gallery and from the goddesses in the stalls, to enjoy the charm of the production, and to take delight in the art. The lions are behind the footlights and not in front of them when we have a noble tragedy nobly acted. And I have rarely witnessed such enthusiasm as that which greeted on last Saturday night the two artists I have mentioned. I would like, in fact, to use the word ovation, but a pedantic professor has recently informed us, with the Batavian buoyancy of misapplied learning, that this expression is not to be employed except when a sheep has been sacrificed. At the Lyceum last week I need hardly say nothing so dreadful occurred. The only inartistic incident of the evening was the hurling of a bouquet from a box at Mr Irving while he was engaged in pourtraying the agony of Hamlet's death, and the pathos of his parting with Horatio. The Dramatic College might take up the education of spectators as well as that of players, and teach people that there is a proper moment for the throwing of flowers as well as a proper method.

As regards Mr Irving's own performance, it has been already so elaborately criticized and described, from his business with the supposed pictures in the closet scene down to his use of 'peacock' for 'paddock', that little remains to be said; nor, indeed, does a Lyceum audience require the interposition of the dramatic critic in order to understand or to appreciate the Hamlet of this great actor. I call him a great actor because he brings to the interpretation of a work of art the two qualities which we in this century so much desire, the qualities of personality and of perfection. A few years ago it seemed to many, and perhaps rightly, that the personality overshadowed the art. No such criticism would be fair now. The somewhat harsh angularity of movement and faulty pronunciation have been replaced by exquisite grace of gesture and clear precision of word, where such precision is necessary. For delightful as good elocution is, few things are so depressing as to hear a passionate passage recited instead of being acted. The quality of a fine performance is its life more than its learning, and every word in a play has a musical as well as an intellectual value, and must be made expressive of a certain emotion. So it does not seem to me that in all parts of a play perfect pronunciation is necessarily dramatic. When the words are 'wild and whirling', the expression of them must be wild and whirling also. Mr Irving, I think, manages his voice with singular art; it was impossible to discern a false note or wrong intonation in his dialogue or his soliloquies, and his strong dramatic power, his realistic power as an actor, is as effective as ever. A great critic at the beginning of this century said that Hamlet is the most difficult part to personate on the stage, that it is like the attempt to 'embody a shadow'. I cannot say that I agree with this idea. Hamlet seems to me essentially a good acting part, and in Mr Irving's performance of it there is that combination of poetic grace with absolute reality which is so eternally delightful. Indeed, if the words easy and difficult have any meaning at all in matters of art, I would be inclined to say that Ophelia is the more difficult part. She has, I mean, less material by which to produce her effects. She is the occasion of the tragedy, but she is neither its heroine nor its chief victim. She is swept away by circumstances, and gives the opportunity for situation, of which she is not herself the climax, and which she does not herself command. And of all the parts which Miss Terry has acted in her brilliant career, there is none in which her infinite powers of pathos and her imaginative and creative faculty are more shown than in her Ophelia. Miss

Terry is one of those rare artists who needs for her dramatic effect no elaborate dialogue, and for whom the simplest words are sufficient. 'I love you not,' says Hamlet, and all that Ophelia answers is, 'I was the more deceived.' These are not very grand words to read, but as Miss Terry gave them in acting they seemed to be the highest possible expression of Ophelia's character. Beautiful, too, was the quick remorse she conveyed by her face and gesture the moment she had lied to Hamlet and told him her father was at home. This I thought a masterpiece of good acting, and her mad scene was wonderful beyond all description. The secrets of Melpomene are known to Miss Terry as well as the secrets of Thalia. As regards the rest of the company there is always a high standard at the Lyceum, but some particular mention should be made of Mr Alexander's brilliant performance of Laertes. Mr Alexander has a most effective presence, a charming voice, and a capacity for wearing lovely costumes with ease and elegance. Indeed, in the latter respect his only rival was Mr Norman Forbes, who played either Guildenstern or Rosencrantz very gracefully. I believe one of our budding Hazlitts is preparing a volume to be entitled 'Great Guildensterns and Remarkable Rosencrantzes,' but I have never been able myself to discern any difference between these two characters. They are, I think, the only characters Shakespeare has not cared to individualize. Whichever of the two, however, Mr Forbes acted, he acted it well. Only one point in Mr Alexander's performance seemed to me open to question, that was his kneeling during the whole of Polonius's speech. For this I see no necessity at all, and it makes the scene look less natural than it should – gives it, I mean, too formal an air. However, the performance was most spirited and gave great pleasure to every one. Mr Alexander is an artist from whom much will be expected, and I have no doubt he will give us much that is fine and noble. He seems to have all the qualifications for a good actor.

There is just one other character I should like to notice. The First Player seemed to me to act far too well. He should act very badly. The First Player, besides his position in the dramatic evolution of the tragedy, is Shakespeare's caricature of the ranting actor of his day, just as the passage he recites is Shakespeare's own parody on the dull plays of some of his rivals. The whole point of Hamlet's advice to the players seems to me to be lost unless the Player himself has been guilty of the fault which Hamlet reprehends, unless he has sawn the air with his hand, mouthed his lines, torn his passion to tatters, and out-Heroded Herod. The very sensibility which Hamlet notices in the actor, such as his real tears and the like, is not the quality of a good artist. The part should be played after the manner of a provincial tragedian. It is meant to be a satire, and to play it well is to play it badly. The scenery and costumes were excellent with the exception of the King's dress, which was coarse in colour and tawdry in effect. And the Player Queen should have come in boy's attire to Elsinore.

However, last Saturday night was not a night for criticism. The theatre was filled with those who desired to welcome Mr Irving back to his own theatre, and we were all delighted at his reappearance among us. I hope that some time will elapse before he and Miss Terry cross again that disappointing Atlantic Ocean.

Henry the Fourth
at Oxford

Dramatic Review, 23 May 1885

I have been told that the ambition of every Dramatic Club is to act *Henry IV*. I am not surprised. The spirit of comedy is as fervent in this play as is the spirit of chivalry; it is an heroic pageant as well as an heroic poem, and like most of Shakespeare's historical dramas it contains an extraordinary number of thoroughly good acting parts, each of which is absolutely individual in character, and each of which contributes to the evolution of the plot.

Rumour, from time to time, has brought in tidings of a proposed production by the banks of the Cam, but it seems at the last moment *Box and Cox* has always had to be substituted in the bill.

To Oxford belongs the honour of having been the first to present on the stage this noble play, and the production which I saw last week was in every way worthy of that lovely town, that mother of sweetness and of light. For, in spite of the roaring of the young lions at the Union, and the screaming of the rabbits in the home of the vivisector, in spite of Keble College, and the tramways, and the sporting prints, Oxford still remains the most beautiful thing in England, and nowhere else are life and art so exquisitely blended, so perfectly made one. Indeed, in most other towns art has often to present herself in the form of a reaction against the sordid ugliness of ignoble lives, but at Oxford she comes to us as an exquisite flower born of the beauty of life and expressive of life's joy. She finds her home by the Isis as once she did by the Ilissus; the Magdalen walks and the Magdalen cloisters are as dear to her as were ever the silver olives of Colonus and the golden gateway of the house of Pallas: she covers with fanlike tracery the vaulted entrance to Christ Church

Hall, and looks out from the windows of Merton; her feet have stirred the Cumnor cowslips, and she gathers fritillaries in the river-fields. To her the clamour of the schools and the dulness of the lecture-room are a weariness and a vexation of spirit; she seeks not to define virtue, and cares little for the categories; she smiles on the swift athlete whose plastic grace has pleased her, and rejoices in the young Barbarians at their games; she watches the rowers from the reedy bank and gives myrtle to her lovers, and laurel to her poets, and rue to those who talk wisely in the street; she makes the earth lovely to all who dream with Keats; she opens high heaven to all who soar with Shelley; and turning away her head from pedant, proctor and Philistine, she has welcomed to her shrine a band of youthful actors, knowing that they have sought with much ardour for the stern secret of Melpomene, and caught with much gladness the sweet laughter of Thalia. And to me this ardour and this gladness were the two most fascinating qualities of the Oxford performance, as indeed they are qualities which are necessary to any fine dramatic production. For without quick and imaginative observation of life the most beautiful play becomes dull in presentation, and what is not conceived in delight by the actor can give no delight at all to others.

I know that there are many who consider that Shakespeare is more for the study than for the stage. With this view I do not for a moment agree. Shakespeare wrote the plays to be acted, and we have no right to alter the form which he himself selected for the full expression of his work. Indeed, many of the beauties of that work can be adequately conveyed to us only through the actor's art. As I sat in the Town Hall of Oxford the other night, the majesty of the mighty lines of the play seemed to me to gain new music from the clear young voices that uttered them, and the ideal grandeur of the heroism to be made more real to the spectators by the chivalrous bearing, the noble gesture and the fine passion of its exponents. Even the dresses had their dramatic value. Their archaeological accuracy gave us, immediately on the rise of the curtain, a perfect picture of the time. As the knights and nobles moved across the stage in the flowing robes of peace and in the burnished steel of battle, we needed no dreary chorus to tell us in what age or land the play's action was passing, for the fifteenth century in all the dignity and grace of its apparel was living actually before us, and the delicate harmonies of colour struck from the first a dominant note of beauty which added to the intellectual realism of archaeology the sensuous charm of art.

As for individual actors, Mr Mackinnon's Prince Hal was a most gay and graceful performance, lit here and there with charming touches of princely dignity and of noble feeling. Mr Coleridge's Falstaff was full of delightful humour, though perhaps at times he did not take us sufficiently into his confidence. An audience looks at a tragedian, but a comedian looks at his audience. However, he gave much pleasure to every one, and Mr Bourchier's Hotspur was really most remarkable. Mr Bourchier has a fine stage presence, a beautiful voice, and produces his effects by a method as dramatically impressive as it is artistically right. Once or twice he seemed to me to spoil his last line by walking through it. The part of Harry Percy is one full of climaxes which must not be let slip. But still there was always a freedom and spirit in his style which was very pleasing, and his delivery of the colloquial passages I thought excellent, notably of that in the first act:

> What d'ye call the place?
> A plague upon't – it is in Gloucestershire;
> 'Twas where the madcap duke his uncle kept,
> His uncle York;

lines by the way in which Kemble made a great effect. Mr Bourchier has the opportunity of a fine career on the English stage, and I hope he will take advantage of it. Among the minor parts in the play Glendower, Mortimer and Sir Richard Vernon were capitally acted, Worcester was a performance of some subtlety, Mrs Woods was a charming Lady Percy, and Lady Edward Spencer Churchill, as Mortimer's wife, made us all believe that we understood Welsh. Her dialogue and her song were most pleasing bits of artistic realism which fully accounted for the Celtic chair at Oxford.

But though I have mentioned particular actors, the real value of the whole representation was to be found in its absolute unity, in its delicate sense of proportion, and in that breadth of effect which is to be got only by the most careful elaboration of detail. I have rarely seen a production better stage-managed. Indeed, I hope that the University will take some official notice of this delightful work of art. Why should not degrees be granted for good acting? Are they not given to those who misunderstand Plato and who mistranslate Aristotle? And should the artist be passed over? No. To Prince Hal, Hotspur and Falstaff, D.C.L.s should be gracefully offered. I feel sure they would be gracefully accepted. To the rest of the company the crimson or the sheep-skin hood might be assigned *honoris causa* to the eternal confusion of the Philistine, and the rage of the industrious and the dull. Thus would Oxford confer honour on herself, and the artist be placed in his proper position. However, whether or not Convocation recognizes the claims of culture, I hope that the Oxford Dramatic Society will produce every summer for us some noble play like *Henry IV*. For, in plays of this kind, plays which deal with bygone times, there is always this peculiar charm, that they combine in one exquisite presentation the passions that are living with the picturesqueness that is dead. And when we have the modern spirit given to us in an antique form, the very remoteness of that form can be made a method of increased realism. This was Shakespeare's own attitude towards the ancient world, this is the attitude we in this century should adopt towards his plays, and with a feeling akin to this it seemed to me that these brilliant young Oxonians were working. If it was so, their aim is the right one. For while we look to the dramatist to give romance to realism, we ask of the actor to give realism to romance.

Aristotle at Afternoon Tea

Pall Mall Gazette, 16 December 1887

In society, says Mr Mahaffy, every civilized man and woman ought to feel it their duty to say something, even when there is hardly anything to be said, and, in order to encourage this delightful art of brilliant chatter, he has published a social guide without which no *débutante* or dandy should ever dream of going out to dine. Not that Mr Mahaffy's book can be said to be, in any sense of the word, popular. In discussing this important subject of conversation, he has not merely followed the scientific method of Aristotle which is, perhaps, excusable, but he has adopted the literary style of Aristotle for which no excuse is possible. There is, also, hardly a single anecdote, hardly a single illustration, and the reader is left to put the Professor's abstract rules into practice, without either the examples or the warnings of history to encourage or to dissuade him in his reckless career. Still, the book can be warmly recommended to all who propose to substitute the vice of verbosity for the stupidity of silence. It fascinates in spite of its form and pleases in spite of its pedantry, and is the nearest approach, that we know of, in modern literature to meeting Aristotle at an afternoon tea.

As regards physical conditions, the only one that is considered by Mr Mahaffy as being absolutely essential to a good conversationalist, is the possession of a musical voice. Some learned writers have been of opinion that a slight stammer often gives peculiar zest to conversation, but Mr Mahaffy rejects this view and is extremely severe on every eccentricity from a native brogue to an artificial catchword. With his remarks on the latter point, the meaningless repetition of phrases, we entirely agree. Nothing can be more irritating than the scientific person who is always saying '*Exactly so,*' or the commonplace person who ends every sentence with '*Don't you know?*' or the pseudo-artistic person who murmurs '*Charming, charming,*' on the smallest provocation. It is, however, with the mental and moral qualifications for conversation that Mr Mahaffy specially deals. Knowledge he, naturally, regards as an absolute essential, for, as he most justly observes, 'an ignorant man is seldom agreeable, except as a butt.' Upon the other hand, strict accuracy should be avoided. 'Even a consummate liar,' says Mr Mahaffy, is a better ingredient in a company than 'the scrupulously truthful man, who weighs every statement, questions every fact, and corrects every inaccuracy.' The liar at any rate recognizes that recreation, not instruction, is the aim of conversation, and is a far more civilized being than the blockhead who loudly expresses his disbelief in a story which is told simply for the amusement of the company. Mr Mahaffy, however, makes an exception in favour of the eminent specialist and tells us that intelligent questions addressed to an astronomer, or a pure mathematician, will elicit many curious facts which will pleasantly beguile the time. Here, in the interest of Society, we feel bound to enter a formal protest. Nobody, even in the provinces, should ever be allowed to ask an intelligent question about pure mathematics across a dinner table. A question of this kind is quite as bad as enquiring suddenly about the state of a man's soul, a sort of *coup* which, as Mr Mahaffy remarks elsewhere, 'many pious people have actually thought a decent introduction to a conversation'.

As for the moral qualifications of a good talker, Mr Mahaffy, following the example of his great master, warns us against any disproportionate excess of virtue. Modesty, for instance, may easily become a social vice, and to be continually apologizing for one's ignorance or stupidity is a grave injury to conversation, for, 'what we want to learn from each member is his free opinion on the subject in hand, not his own estimate of the value of that opinion.' Simplicity, too, is not without its dangers. The *enfant terrible*, with his shameless love of truth, the raw country-bred girl who always says what she means, and the plain, blunt man who makes a point of speaking his mind on every possible occasion, without ever considering whether he has a mind at all, are the fatal examples of what simplicity leads to. Shyness may be a form of vanity, and reserve a development of pride, and as for sympathy, what can be more detestable than the man, or woman, who insists on agreeing with everybody, and so makes 'a discussion, which implies differences in opinion', absolutely impossible? Even the unselfish listener is apt to become a bore. 'These silent people,' says Mr Mahaffy, 'not only take all they can get in Society for nothing, but they take it without the smallest gratitude, and have the audacity afterwards to censure those who have laboured for their amusement.' Tact, which is an exquisite sense of the symmetry of things, is, according to Mr Mahaffy, the highest and best of all the moral conditions for conversation. The man of tact, he most wisely remarks, 'will instinctively avoid jokes about Blue Beard' in the company of a woman who is a man's third wife; he will never be guilty of talking like a book, but will rather avoid too careful an attention to grammar and the rounding of periods; he will cultivate the art of graceful interruption, so as to prevent a subject being worn threadbare by the aged or the inexperienced; and should he be desirous of telling a story, he will look round and consider each member of the party, and if there be a single stranger present will forgo the pleasure of anecdotage rather than make the social mistake of hurting even one of the guests. As for prepared or premeditated art, Mr Mahaffy has a great contempt for it and tells us of a certain college don (let us hope not at Oxford or Cambridge) who always carried a jest-book in his pocket and had to refer to it when he wished to make a repartee. Great wits, too, are often very cruel, and great humorists often very vulgar, so it will be better to try and 'make good conversation without any large help from these brilliant but dangerous gifts.'

In a *tête-à-tête* one should talk about persons, and in general society about things. The state of the weather is always an excusable exordium, but it is convenient to have a paradox or heresy on the subject always ready so as to direct the conversation into other channels. Really domestic people are almost invariably bad talkers as their very virtues in home life have dulled their interest in outer things. The very best mothers will insist on chattering of their babies and prattling about infant education. In fact, most women do not take sufficient interest in politics, just as most men are deficient in general reading. Still, anybody can be made to talk, except the very obstinate, and even a commercial traveller may be drawn out and become quite interesting. As for Society small talk, it is impossible, Mr Mahaffy tells us, for any sound theory of conversation to depreciate gossip, 'which is perhaps the main factor in agreeable talk throughout Society.' The retailing of small personal points about great people always gives pleasure, and if one is not fortunate enough to be an Arctic traveller or an escaped Nihilist, the best thing one can do is to relate some anecdote of 'Prince Bismarck, or King Victor Emmanuel, or Mr Gladstone'. In the case of meeting a genius and a Duke at dinner, the good talker will try to raise himself to the level of the former and to bring the latter down to his own level. To succeed among one's social superiors one must have no hesitation in contradicting them. Indeed, one should make bold criticisms and introduce a bright and free tone into a Society whose grandeur and extreme respectability make it, Mr Mahaffy remarks, as pathetically as inaccurately, 'perhaps somewhat dull'. The best conversationalists are those whose ancestors have been bilingual, like the French and Irish, but the art of conversation is really within the reach of almost every one, except those who are morbidly truthful, or whose high moral worth requires to be sustained by a permanent gravity of demeanour and a general dulness of mind.

These are the broad principles contained in Mr Mahaffy's clever little book, and many of them will, no doubt, commend themselves to our readers. The maxim, 'If you find the company dull, blame yourself,' seems to us somewhat optimistic, and we have no sympathy at all with the professional storyteller who is really a great bore at a dinner table; but Mr Mahaffy is quite right in insisting that no bright social intercourse is possible without equality, and it is no objection to his book to say that it will not teach people how to talk cleverly. It is not logic that makes men reasonable, nor the science of ethics that makes men good, but it is always useful to analyse, to formularize and to investigate. The only thing to be regretted in the volume is the arid and jejune character of the style. If Mr Mahaffy would only write as he talks, his book would be much pleasanter reading.

The Principles of the Art of Conversation: A Social Essay. By J. P. Mahaffy. (Macmillan and Co.)

Injury and Insult

from A Batch of Novels

Pall Mall Gazette, 2 May 1887

O f the three great Russian novelists of our time Turgenev is
by far the finest artist. He has that spirit of exquisite
selection, that delicate choice of detail, which is the essence of
style; his work is entirely free from any personal intention; and
by taking existence at its most fiery-coloured moments he can
distil into a few pages of perfect prose the moods and passions
of many lives.

Count Tolstoi's method is much larger, and his field of vision
more extended. He reminds us sometimes of Paul Veronese, and,
like that great painter, can crowd, without overcrowding, the
giant canvas on which he works. We may not at first gain from
his works that artistic unity of impression which is Turgenev's
chief charm, but once we have mastered the details the whole
seems to have the grandeur and the simplicity of an epic. Dostoyevsky differs widely from both his rivals. He is not so fine an
artist as Turgenev, for he deals more with the facts than with
the effects of life; nor has he Tolstoi's largeness of vision and
epic dignity; but he has qualities that are distinctively and absolutely his own, such as a fierce intensity of passion and concentration of impulse, a power of dealing with the deepest mysteries
of psychology and the most hidden springs of life, and a realism
that is pitiless in its fidelity, and terrible because it is true. Some
time ago we had occasion to draw attention to his marvellous
novel *Crime and Punishment*, where in the haunt of impurity and
vice a harlot and an assassin meet together to read the story of
Dives and Lazarus, and the outcast girl leads the sinner to make
atonement for his sin; nor is the book entitled *Injury and Insult* at
all inferior to that great masterpiece. Mean and ordinary though
the surroundings of the story may seem, the heroine Natasha is

like one of the noble victims of Greek tragedy; she is Antigone
with the passion of Phaedra, and it is impossible to approach
her without a feeling of awe. Greek also is the gloom of Nemesis
that hangs over each character; only it is a Nemesis that does
not stand outside life, but is part of our own nature and of the
same material as life itself – Aleosha, the beautiful young lad
whom Natasha follows to her doom, is a second Titus Melema,
and has all Tito's grace and fascination. Yet he is different. He
would never have denied Baldassare in the Square at Florence,
nor lied to Romula about Tessa. He has a magnificent, momentary sincerity, a boyish unconsciousness of all that life signifies,
an ardent enthusiasm for all that life cannot give. There is
nothing calculating about him. He never thinks evil, he only does
it. From a psychological point of view he is one of the most
interesting characters of modern fiction, as from an artistic he is
one of the most attractive. As we grow to know him he stirs
strange questions for us, and makes us feel that it is not the
wicked only who do wrong, nor the bad alone who work evil.

And by what a subtle objective method does Dostoyevsky show
us his characters! He never tickets them with a list or labels
them with a description. We grow to know them very gradually,
as we know people whom we meet in society, at first by little
tricks of manner, personal appearance, fancies in dress, and the
like; and afterwards by their deeds and words; and even then
they constantly elude us, for though Dostoyevsky may lay bare
for us the secrets of their nature, yet he never explains his personages away; they are always surprising us by something that they
say or do, and keep to the end the eternal mystery of life.

Irrespective of its value as a work of art, this novel possesses
a deep autobiographical interest also, as the character of Vania,
the poor student who loves Natasha through all her sins and
shame, is Dostoyevsky's study of himself. Goethe once had to
delay the completion of one of his novels till experience had
furnished him with new situations, but almost before he had
arrived at manhood Dostoyevsky knew life in its most real forms;
poverty and suffering, pain and misery, prison, exile, and love,
were soon familiar to him, and by the lips of Vania he has told
his own story. This note of personal feeling, this harsh reality of

actual experience, undoubtedly gives the book something of its strange fervour and terrible passion, yet it has not made it egotistic; we see things from every point of view, and we feel, not that fiction has been trammelled by fact, but that fact itself has become ideal and imaginative. Pitiless, too, though Dostoyevsky is in his method as an artist, as a man he is full of human pity for all, for those who do evil as well as for those who suffer for it, for the selfish no less than for those whose lives are wrecked for others and whose sacrifice is in vain. Since *Adam Bede* and *Le Père Goriot* no more powerful novel has been written than *Injury and Insult*.

Injury and Insult By Fedor Dostoyevsky.
Translated from the Russian by Frederick Whishaw. (Vizetelly and Co.)

Great Writers by Little Men

Pall Mall Gazette, 28 March 1887

In an introductory note prefixed to the initial volume of 'Great
Writers', a series of literary monographs now being issued by
Mr Walter Scott, the publisher himself comes forward in the
kindest manner possible to give his authors the requisite 'puff
preliminary', and ventures to express the modest opinion that
such original and valuable works 'have never before been produced in any part of the world at a price so low as a shilling a
volume.' Far be it from us to make any heartless allusion to the
fact that Shakespeare's *Sonnets* were brought out at fivepence, or
that for fourpence-halfpenny one could have bought a Martial
in ancient Rome. Every man, a cynical American tells us, has
the right to beat a drum before his booth. Still, we must acknowledge that Mr Walter Scott would have been much better
employed in correcting some of the more obvious errors that
appear in his series. When, for instance, we come across such a
phrase as 'the brotherly liberality of the brothers *Wedgewood*', the
awkwardness of the expression is hardly atoned for by the fact
that the name of the great potter is misspelt; Longfellow is so
essentially poor in rhymes that it is unfair to rob him even of
one, and the misquotation on page 77 is absolutely unkind; the
joke Coleridge himself made upon the subject should have been
sufficient to remind any one that 'Comberbach' (*sic*) was not the
name under which he enlisted, and no real beauty is added to
the first line of his pathetic *Work Without Hope* by printing 'lare'
(*sic*) instead of 'lair'. The truth is that all premature panegyrics
bring their own punishment upon themselves and, in the present
case, though the series has only just entered upon existence,
already a great deal of the work done is careless, disappointing,
unequal and tedious.

Mr Eric Robertson's *Longfellow* is a most depressing book. No one survives being overestimated, nor is there any surer way of destroying an author's reputation than to glorify him without judgement and to praise him without tact. Henry Wadsworth Longfellow was one of the first true men of letters America produced, and as such deserves a high place in any history of American civilization. To a land out of breath in its greed for gain he showed the example of a life devoted entirely to the study of literature; his lectures, though not by any means brilliant, were still productive of much good; he had a most charming and gracious personality, and he wrote some pretty poems. But his poems are not of the kind that call for intellectual analysis or for elaborate description or, indeed, for any serious discussion at all. They are as unsuited for panegyric as they are unworthy of censure, and it is difficult to help smiling when Mr Robertson gravely tells us that few modern poets have given utterance to a faith so comprehensive as that expressed in the *Psalm of Life*, or that *Evangeline* should confer on Longfellow the title of 'Golden-mouthed', and that the style of metre adopted 'carries the ear back to times in the world's history when grand simplicities were sung.' Surely Mr Robertson does not believe that there is any connection at all between Longfellow's unrhymed dactylics and the hexameter of Greece and Rome, or that any one reading *Evangeline* would be reminded of Homer's or Virgil's line? Where also lies the advantage of confusing popularity with poetic power? Though the *Psalm of Life* be shouted from Maine to California, that would not make it true poetry. Why call upon us to admire a bad misquotation from the *Midnight Mass for the Dying Year*, and why talk of Longfellow's 'hundreds of imitators'? Longfellow has no imitators, for of echoes themselves there are no echoes and it is only style that makes a school.

Now and then, however, Mr Robertson considers it necessary to assume a critical attitude. He tells us, for instance, that whether or not Longfellow was a genius of the first order, it must be admitted that he loved social pleasures and was a good eater and judge of wines, admiring 'Bass's ale' more than anything else he had seen in England! The remarks on *Excelsior* are even still more amazing. *Excelsior*, says Mr Robertson, is not a ballad because a ballad deals either with real or with supernatural people, and the hero of the poem cannot be brought under either category. For, 'were he of human flesh, his madcap notion of scaling a mountain with the purpose of getting to the sky would be simply drivelling lunacy,' to say nothing of the fact that the peak in question is much frequented by tourists, while, on the other hand, 'it would be absurd to suppose him a spirit . . . for no spirit would be so silly as climb a snowy mountain for nothing'! It is really painful to have to read such preposterous nonsense, and if Mr Walter Scott imagines that work of this kind is 'original and valuable' he has much to learn. Nor are Mr Robertson's criticisms upon other poets at all more felicitous. The casual allusion to Herrick's 'confectioneries of verse' is, of course, quite explicable, coming as it does from an editor who excluded Herrick from an anthology of the child-poems of our literature in favour of Mr Ashby-Sterry and Mr William Sharp, but when Mr Robertson tells us that Poe's 'loftiest flights of imagination in verse . . . rise into no more empyreal realm than the *fantastic*,' we can only recommend him to read as soon as possible the marvellous lines *To Helen*, a poem as beautiful as a Greek gem and as musical as Apollo's lute. The remarks, too, on Poe's critical estimate of his own work show that Mr Robertson has never really studied the poet on whom he pronounces such glib and shallow judgements, and exemplify very clearly the fact that even dogmatism is no excuse for ignorance.

After reading Mr Hall Caine's *Coleridge* we are irresistibly reminded of what Wordsworth once said about a bust that had been done of himself. After contemplating it for some time, he remarked, 'It is not a bad Wordsworth, but it is not the real Wordsworth; it is not Wordsworth the poet, it is the sort of Wordsworth who might be Chancellor of the Exchequer.' Mr Caine's Coleridge is certainly not the sort of Coleridge who might have been Chancellor of the Exchequer, for the author of *Christabel* was not by any means remarkable as a financier; but, for all that, it is not the real Coleridge, it is not Coleridge the poet. The incidents of the life are duly recounted; the gunpowder plot at Cambridge, the egg-hot and oronokoo at the little tavern in Newgate Street, the blue coat and white waistcoat that so amazed the worthy Unitarians, and the terrible smoking experiment at Birmingham are all carefully chronicled, as no doubt they should be in every popular biography; but of the spiritual progress of the man's soul we hear absolutely nothing. Never for one single instant are we brought near to Coleridge; the magic of that wonderful personality is hidden from us by a cloud of mean details, an unholy jungle of facts, and the 'critical history' promised to us by Mr Walter Scott in his unfortunate preface is conspicuous only by its absence.

Carlyle once proposed in jest to write a life of Michelangelo without making any reference to his art, and Mr Caine has shown that such a project is perfectly feasible. He has written the life of a great peripatetic philosopher and chronicled only the peripatetics. He has tried to tell us about a poet, and his book might be the biography of the famous tallow-chandler who would not appreciate the *Watchman*. The real events of Coleridge's life are not his gig excursions and his walking tours; they are his thoughts, dreams and passions, his moments of creative impulse, their source and secret, his moods of imaginative joy, their marvel and their meaning, and not his moods merely but the music and the melancholy that they brought him; the lyric loveliness of his voice when he sang, the sterile sorrow of the years when he was silent. It is said that every man's life is a Soul's Tragedy. Coleridge's certainly was so, and though we may not be able to pluck out the heart of his mystery, still let us recognize that mystery is there; and that the goings-out and comings-in of a man, his places of sojourn and his roads of travel are but idle things to chronicle, if that which is the man be left unrecorded. So mediocre is Mr Caine's book that even accuracy could not make it better.

On the whole, then, Mr Walter Scott cannot be congratulated on the success of his venture so far. The one really admirable feature of the series is the bibliography that is appended to each volume. These bibliographies are compiled by Mr Anderson, of the British Museum, and are so valuable to the student, as well as interesting in themselves, that it is much to be regretted that they should be accompanied by such tedious letterpress.

1 *Life of Henry Wadsworth Longfellow*. By Eric S. Robertson.

2 *Life of Samuel Taylor Coleridge*. By Hall Caine. Both 'Great Writers' Series. (Walter Scott.)

A Cheap Edition
of a Great Man

Pall Mall Gazette, 18 April 1887

Formerly we used to canonize our great men; nowadays we vulgarize them. The vulgarization of Rossetti has been going on for some time past with really remarkable success, and there seems no probability at present of the process being discontinued. The grass was hardly green upon the quiet grave in Birchington churchyard when Mr Hall Caine and Mr William Sharp rushed into print with their Memoirs and Recollections. Then came the usual mob of magazine-hacks with their various views and attitudes, and now Mr Joseph Knight has produced for the edification of the British public a popular biography of the poet of the Blessed Damozel, the painter of Dante's Dream.

It is only fair to state that Mr Knight's work is much better than that of his predecessors in the same field. His book is, on the whole, modestly and simply written; whatever its other faults may be, it is at least free from affectation of any kind; and it makes no serious pretence at being either exhaustive or definitive. Yet the best we can say of it is that it is just the sort of biography Guildenstern might have written of Hamlet. Nor does its unsatisfactory character come merely from the ludicrous inadequacy of the materials at Mr Knight's disposal; it is the whole scheme and method of the book that is radically wrong. Rossetti's was a great personality, and personalities such as his do not easily survive shilling primers. Sooner or later they have inevitably to come down to the level of their biographers, and in the present instance nothing could be more absolutely commonplace than the picture Mr Knight gives us of the wonderful seer and singer whose life he has so recklessly essayed to write.

No doubt there are many people who will be deeply interested to know that Rossetti was once chased round his garden by an

infuriated zebu he was trying to exhibit to Mr Whistler, or that
he had a great affection for a dog called 'Dizzy', or that 'sloshy'
was one of his favourite words of contempt, or that Mr Gosse
thought him very like Chaucer in appearance, or that he had
'an absolute disqualification' for whist-playing, or that he was
very fond of quoting the *Bab Ballads*, or that he once said that if
he could live by writing poetry he would see painting d —— d!
For our part, however, we cannot help expressing our regret that
such a shallow and superficial biography as this should ever have
been published. It is but a sorry task to rip the twisted ravel
from the worn garment of life and to turn the grout in a drained
cup. Better, after all, that we knew a painter only through his
vision and a poet through his song, than that the image of a
great man, should be marred and made mean for us by the
clumsy geniality of good intentions. A true artist, and such Rossetti undoubtedly was, reveals himself so perfectly in his work,
that unless a biographer has something more valuable to give us
than idle anecdotes and unmeaning tales, his labour is misspent
and his industry misdirected.

Bad, however, as is Mr Knight's treatment of Rossetti's life,
his treatment of Rossetti's poetry is infinitely worse. Considering
the small size of the volume, and the consequently limited
number of extracts, the amount of misquotation is almost incred-
ible, and puts all recent achievements in this sphere of modern
literature completely into the shade. The fine line in the first
canto of *Rose Mary*:

What glints there like a lance that flees?

appears as:

What glints there like a *glance* that flees?

which is very painful nonsense; in the description of that graceful
and fanciful sonnet *Autumn Idleness*, the deer are represented as
'*grazing* from hillock eaves' instead of gazing from hillock-eaves;
the opening of *Dantis Tenebrae* is rendered quite incomprehensible
by the substitution of 'my' for 'thy' in the second line; even such
a well-known ballad as *Sister Helen* is misquoted, and indeed,
from the *Burden of Nineveh*, the *Blessed Damozel*, the *King's Tragedy*

and Guido Cavalcanti's lovely *ballata*, down to the *Portrait* and such sonnets as *Love-sweetness*, *Farewell to the Glen*, and *A Match with the Moon*, there is not one single poem that does not display some careless error or some stupid misprint.

As for Rossetti's elaborate system of punctuation, Mr Knight pays no attention to it whatsoever. Indeed, he shows quite a rollicking indifference to all the secrets and subtleties of style, and inserts or removes stops in a manner that is absolutely destructive to the lyrical beauty of the verse. The hyphen, also, so constantly employed by Rossetti in the case of such expressions as 'hillock-eaves' quoted above, 'hill-fire', 'birth-hour,' and the like, is almost invariably disregarded, and by the brilliant omission of a semicolon Mr Knight has succeeded in spoiling one of the best stanzas in *The Staff and Scrip* – a poem, by the way, that he speaks of as *The Staff and the Scrip* (*sic*). After this tedious comedy of errors it seems almost unnecessary to point out that the earliest Italian poet is not called Ciullo *D'Alcano* (*sic*), or that *The Bothie of Toper-na-Fuosich* (*sic*) is not the title of Clough's boisterous epic, or that *Dante and his Cycle* (*sic*) is not the name Rossetti gave to his collection of translations; and why *Troy Town* should appear in the index as *Tory Town* is really quite inexplicable, unless it is intended as a compliment to Mr Hall Caine who once dedicated, or rather tried to dedicate, to Rossetti a lecture on the relations of poets to politics. We are sorry, too, to find an English dramatic critic misquoting Shakespeare, as we had always been of the opinion that this was a privilege reserved specially for our English actors.

We sincerely hope that there will soon be an end to all biographies of this kind. They rob life of much of its dignity and its wonder, add to death itself a new terror, and make one wish that all art were anonymous. Nor could there have been any more unfortunate choice of a subject for popular treatment than that to which we owe the memoir that now lies before us. A pillar of fire to the few who knew him, and of cloud to the many who knew him not, Dante Gabriel Rossetti lived apart from the gossip and tittle-tattle of a shallow age. He never trafficked with the merchants for his soul, nor brought his wares into the market-place for the idle to gape at. Passionate and romantic though he was, yet there was in his nature something of high austerity. He loved seclusion, and hated notoriety, and would have shuddered at the idea that within a few years after his death he was to make his appearance in a series of popular biographies, sandwiched between the author of *Pickwick* and the Great Lexicographer. One man alone, the friend his verse won for him, did he desire should write his life, and it is to Mr Theodore Watts that we, too, must look to give us the real Rossetti. It may be admitted at once that Mr Watts's subject has for the moment been a little spoiled for him. Rude hands have touched it, and unmusical voices have made it sound almost common in our ears. Yet none the less is it for him to tell us of the marvel of this man whose art he has analysed with such exquisite insight, whose life he knows as no one else can know it, whom he so loyally loved and tended, and by whom he was so loyally beloved in turn. As for the others, the scribblers and nibblers of literature, if they indeed reverence Rossetti's memory, let them pay him the one homage he would most have valued, the gracious homage of silence. 'Though you can fret me, yet you cannot play upon me,' says Hamlet to his false friend, and even so might Rossetti speak to those well-intentioned mediocrities who would seem to know his stops and would sound him to the top of his compass. True, they cannot fret him now, for he has passed beyond the possibility of pain; yet they cannot play upon him either; it is not for them to pluck out the heart of his mystery.

There is, however, one feature of this book that deserves unstinted praise. Mr Anderson's bibliography will be found of immense use by every student of Rossetti's work and influence. Perhaps Young's very powerful attack on Pre-Raphaelitism, as expounded by Mr Ruskin (Longmans, 1857), might be included, but, in all other respects, it seems quite complete, and the chronological list of paintings and drawings is really admirable. When this unfortunate 'Great Writers' Series comes to an end, Mr Anderson's bibliographies should be collected together and published in a separate volume. At present they are in a very second-rate company indeed.

Life of Dante Gabriel Rossetti. By Joseph Knight. 'Great Writers' Series. (Walter Scott.)

Two Biographies of Keats

Pall Mall Gazette, 27 September 1887

'Apoet,' said Keats once, 'is the most unpoetical of all God's creatures,' and whether the aphorism be universally true or not, this is certainly the impression produced by the two last biographies that have appeared of Keats himself. It cannot be said that either Mr Colvin or Mr William Rossetti makes us love Keats more or understand him better. In both these books there is much that is like 'chaff in the mouth', and in Mr Rossetti's there is not a little that is like 'brass on the palate'. To a certain degree this is, no doubt, inevitable nowadays. Everybody pays a penalty for peeping through keyholes, and the keyhole and the backstairs are essential parts of the method of the modern biographers. It is only fair, however, to state at the outset that Mr Colvin has done his work much better than Mr Rossetti. The account Mr Colvin gives of Keats's boyhood, for instance, is very pleasing, and so is the sketch of Keats's circle of friends, both Leigh Hunt and Haydon being admirably drawn. Here and there, trivial family details are introduced without much regard to proportion, and the posthumous panegyrics of devoted friends are not really of so much value, in helping us to form any true estimate of Keats's actual character, as Mr Colvin seems to imagine. We have no doubt that when Bailey wrote to Lord Houghton that common sense and gentleness were Keats's two special characteristics the worthy Archdeacon meant extremely well, but we prefer the real Keats, with his passionate wilfulness, his fantastic moods and his fine inconsistence. Part of Keats's charm as a man is his fascinating incompleteness. We do not want him reduced to a sandpaper smoothness or made perfect by the addition of popular virtues. Still, if Mr Colvin has not given us a very true picture of Keats's character, he has certainly told the story of his life in a pleasant and readable manner. He may not write with the ease and grace of a man of letters, but he is never pretentious and not often pedantic.

Mr Rossetti's book is a great failure. To begin with, Mr Rossetti commits the great mistake of separating the man from the artist. The facts of Keats's life are interesting only when they are shown in their relation to his creative activity. The moment they are isolated they are either uninteresting or painful. Mr Rossetti complains that the early part of Keats's life is uneventful and the latter part depressing, but the fault lies with the biographer, not with the subject.

The book opens with a detailed account of Keats's life, in which he spares us nothing, from what he calls the 'sexual misadventure at Oxford' down to the six weeks' dissipation after the appearance of the *Blackwood* article and the hysterical and morbid ravings of the dying man. No doubt, most if not all of the things Mr Rossetti tells us are facts; but there is neither tact shown in the selection that is made of the facts nor sympathy in the use to which they are put. When Mr Rossetti writes of the man he forgets the poet, and when he criticizes the poet he shows that he does not understand the man. His first error, as we have said, is isolating the life from the work; his second error is his treatment of the work itself. Take, for instance, his criticism of that wonderful *Ode to a Nightingale*, with all its marvellous magic of music, colour and form. He begins by saying that 'the first point of weakness' in the poem is the 'surfeit of mythological allusions', a statement which is absolutely untrue, as out of the eight stanzas of the poem only three contain any mythological allusions at all, and of these not one is either forced or remote. Then coming to the second verse,

Oh for a draught of vintage, that hath been
  Cool'd a long age in the deep-delvèd earth,
Tasting of Flora and the country-green,
  Dance, and Provençal song, and sunburnt mirth!

Mr Rossetti exclaims in a fine fit of 'Blue Ribbon' enthusiasm: 'Surely nobody wants wine as a preparation for enjoying a nightingale's music, whether in a literal or in a fanciful relation'! 'To call wine "the true, the blushful Hippocrene" . . . seems' to him 'both stilted and repulsive'; 'the phrase "with beaded bubbles winking at the brim" is (though picturesque) trivial'; 'the succeeding image, "Not charioted by Bacchus and his pards" ' is 'far worse'; while such an expression as 'light-winged Dryad of the trees' is an obvious pleonasm, for Dryad really means *Oak*-nymph! As for that superb burst of passion,

Thou wast not born for death, immortal Bird!
　No hungry generations tread thee down;
The voice I hear this passing night was heard
　In ancient days by emperor and clown:

Mr Rossetti tells us that it is a palpable, or rather 'palpaple (*sic*) fact that this address . . . is a logical solecism,' as men live longer than nightingales. As Mr Colvin makes very much the same criticism, talking of 'a breach of logic which is also . . . a flaw in the poetry,' it may be worth while to point out to these two last critics of Keats's work that what Keats meant to convey was the contrast between the permanence of beauty and the change and decay of human life, an idea which receives its fullest expression in the *Ode on a Grecian Urn*. Nor do the other poems fare much better at Mr Rossetti's hands. The fine invocation in *Isabella*:

Moan hither, all ye syllables of woe,
　From the deep throat of sad Melpomene!
Through bronzèd lyre in tragic order go,
　And touch the strings into a mystery,

seems to him 'a *fadeur*'; the Indian Bacchante of the fourth book of *Endymion* he calls a 'sentimental and beguiling wine-bibber', and, as for Endymion himself, he declares that he cannot understand 'how his human organism, *with respirative and digestive processes*, continues to exist,' and gives us his own idea of how Keats should have treated the subject. An eminent French critic once exclaimed in despair, '*Je trouve des physiologistes partout!*'; but it has been reserved for Mr Rossetti to speculate on Endymion's digestion, and we readily accord to him all the distinction of the position. Even where Mr Rossetti seeks to praise, he spoils what he praises. To speak of *Hyperion* as 'a monument of Cyclopean architecture in verse' is bad enough, but to call it 'a Stonehenge of reverberance' is absolutely detestable; nor do we learn much about *The Eve of St Mark* by being told that its 'simplicity is full-blooded as well as quaint'. What is the meaning, also, of stating that Keats's *Notes on Shakespeare* are 'somewhat strained and *bloated*'? and is there nothing better to be said of Madeline in *The Eve of St Agnes* than that 'she is made a very charming and lovable figure, *although she does nothing very particular except to undress without looking behind her, and to elope*'? There is no necessity to follow Mr Rossetti any further as he flounders about through the quagmire that he has made for his own feet. A critic who can say that 'not many of Keats's poems are highly admirable' need not be too seriously treated. Mr Rossetti is an industrious man and a painstaking writer, but he entirely lacks the temper necessary for the interpretation of such poetry as was written by John Keats.

It is pleasant to turn again to Mr Colvin, who criticizes always with modesty and often with acumen. We do not agree with him when he accepts Mrs Owens's theory of a symbolic and allegoric meaning underlying *Endymion*; his final judgement on Keats as 'the most Shakespearean spirit that has lived since Shakespeare' is not very fortunate; and we are surprised to find him suggesting, on the evidence of a rather silly story of Severn's, that Sir Walter Scott was privy to the *Blackwood* article. There is nothing, however, about his estimate of the poet's work that is harsh, irritating or uncouth. The true Marcellus of English song has not yet found his Virgil, but Mr Colvin makes a tolerable Statius.

1 *Keats*. By Sidney Colvin. 'English Men of Letters' Series. (Macmillan and Co.)

2 *Life of John Keats*. By William Michael Rossetti. 'Great Writers' Series. (Walter Scott.)

The fragments of which this lecture is composed are taken entirely from the original manuscripts. It is not certain that they all belong to the same lecture, nor that all were written at the same period. Some portions were written in Philadelphia in 1882.

Art and the
Handicraftsman

People often talk as if there was an opposition between what is beautiful and what is useful. There is no opposition to beauty except ugliness: all things are either beautiful or ugly, and utility will be always on the side of the beautiful thing, because beautiful decoration is always on the side of the beautiful thing, because beautiful decoration is always an expression of the use you put a thing to and the value placed on it. No workman will beautifully decorate bad work, nor can you possibly get good handicraftsmen or workmen without having beautiful designs. You should be quite sure of that. If you have poor and worthless designs in any craft or trade you will get poor and worthless workmen only, but the minute you have noble and beautiful designs, then you get men of power and intellect and feeling to work for you. By having good designs you have workmen who work not merely with their hands but with their hearts and heads too; otherwise you will get merely the fool or the loafer to work for you.

That the beauty of life is a thing of no moment, I suppose few people would venture to assert. And yet most civilized people act as if it were of none, and in so doing are wronging both themselves and those that are to come after them. For that beauty which is meant by art is no mere accident of human life which people can take or leave, but a positive necessity of life if we are to live as nature meant us to, that is to say unless we are content to be less than men.

Do not think that the commercial spirit which is the basis of your life and cities here is opposed to art. Who built the beautiful cities of the world but commercial men and commercial men only? Genoa built by its traders, Florence by its bankers, and Venice, most lovely of all, by its noble and honest merchants.

I do not wish you, remember, 'to build a new Pisa', nor to bring 'the life or the decorations of the thirteenth century back again'. 'The circumstances with which you must surround your workmen are those' of modern American life, 'because the designs you have now to ask for from your workmen are such as will make modern' American 'life beautiful'. The art we want is the art based on all the inventions of modern civilization, and to suit all the needs of nineteenth-century life.

Do you think, for instance, that we object to machinery? I tell you we reverence it; we reverence it when it does its proper work, when it relieves man from ignoble and soulless labour, not when it seeks to do that which is valuable only when wrought by the hands and hearts of men. Let us have no machine-made orna-ment at all; it is all bad and worthless and ugly. And let us not mistake the means of civilization for the end of civilization; steam engine, telephone and the like, are all wonderful, but remember that their value depends entirely on the noble uses we make of them, on the noble spirit in which we employ them, not on the things themselves.

It is, no doubt, a great advantage to talk to a man at the Antipodes through a telephone; its advantage depends entirely on the value of what the two men have to say to one another. If one merely shrieks slander through a tube and the other whispers folly into a wire, do not think that anybody is very much ben-efited by the invention.

The train that whirls an ordinary Englishman through Italy at the rate of forty miles an hour and finally sends him home without any memory of that lovely country but that he was cheated by a courier at Rome, or that he got a bad dinner at Verona, does not do him or civilization much good. But that swift legion of fiery-footed engines that bore to the burning ruins of Chicago the loving help and generous treasure of the world was as noble and as beautiful as any golden troop of angels that ever fed the hungry and clothed the naked in the antique times. As beautiful, yes; all machinery may be beautiful when it is undecorated even. Do not seek to decorate it. We cannot but think all good machinery is graceful, also, the line of strength and the line of beauty being one.

Give then, as I said, to your workmen of today the bright and noble surroundings that you can yourself create. Stately and simple architecture for your cities, bright and simple dress for your men and women; those are the conditions of a real artistic movement. For the artist is not concerned primarily with any theory of life but with life itself, with the joy and loveliness that should come daily on eye and ear for a beautiful external world.

But the simplicity must not be barrenness nor the bright colour gaudy. For all beautiful colours are graduated colours, the colours that seem about to pass into one another's realm – colour without tone being like music without harmony, mere discord. Barren architecture, the vulgar and glaring advertisements that desecrate not merely your cities but every rock and river that I have seen yet in America – all this is not enough. A school of design we must have too in each city. It should be a stately and noble building, full of the best examples of the best art of the world. Furthermore, do not put your designers in a barren white-washed room and bid them work in that depressing and colour-less atmosphere as I have seen many of the American schools of design, but give them beautiful surroundings. Because you want to produce a permanent canon and standard of taste in your workman, he must have always by him and before him specimens of the best decorative art of the world, so that you can say to him: 'This is good work. Greek or Italian or Japanese wrought it so many years ago, but it is eternally young because eternally beautiful.' Work in this spirit and you will be sure to be right. Do not copy it, but work with the same love, the same reverence, the same freedom of imagination. You must teach him colour and design, how all beautiful colours are graduated colours and glaring colours the essence of vulgarity. Show him the quality of any beautiful work of nature like the rose, or any beautiful work of art like an Eastern carpet – being merely the exquisite graduation of colour, one tone answering another like the answer-ing chords of a symphony. Teach him how the true designer is not he who makes the design and then colours it, but he who designs in colour, creates in colour, thinks in colour too. Show him how the most gorgeous stained glass windows of Europe are filled with white glass, and the most gorgeous Eastern tapestry with toned colours – the primary colours in both places being set in the white glass, and the tone colours like brilliant jewels set in dusky gold. And then as regards design, show him how the real designer will take first any given limited space, little disk of silver, it may be, like a Greek coin, or wide expanse of fretted ceiling or lordly wall as Tintoret chose at Venice (it does not matter which), and to this limited space – the first condition of decoration being the limitation of the size of the material used – he will give the effect of its being filled with beautiful decoration, filled with it as a golden cup will be filled with wine, so complete that you should not be able to take away anything from it or add anything to it. For from a good piece of design you can take away nothing, nor can you add anything to it, each little bit of design being as absolutely necessary and as vitally important to the whole effect as a note or chord of music is for a sonata of Beethoven.

But I said the effect of its being so filled, because this, again, is of the essence of good design. With a simple spray of leaves and a bird in flight a Japanese artist will give you the impression that he has completely covered with lovely design the reed fan or lacquer cabinet at which he is working, merely because he knows the exact spot in which to place them. All good design depends on the texture of the utensil used and the use you wish to put it to. One of the first things I saw in an American school of design was a young lady painting a romantic moonlight land-scape on a large round dish, and another young lady covering a set of dinner-plates with a series of sunsets of the most remarkable colours. Let your ladies paint moonlight landscapes and sunsets, but do not let them paint them on dinner-plates or dishes. Let them take canvas or paper for such work, but not clay or china. They are merely painting the wrong subjects on the wrong material, that is all. They have not been taught that every material and texture has certain qualities of its own. The design suitable for one is quite wrong for the other, just as the design which you should work on a flat table-cover ought to be quite different from the design you would work on a curtain, for the one will always be straight, the other broken into folds; and the use too one puts the object to should guide one in the choice of design. One does not want to eat one's terrapins off a romantic moonlight nor one's clams off a harrowing sunset. Glory of sun and moon, let them be wrought for us by our landscape artist and be on the walls of the rooms we sit in to remind us of the undying beauty of the sunsets that fade and die, but do not let us eat our soup off them and send them down to the kitchen twice a day to be washed and scrubbed by the handmaid.

All these things are simple enough, yet nearly always forgotten. Your school of design here will teach your girls and your boys, your handicraftsmen of the future (for all your schools of art should be local schools, the schools of particular cities). We talk of the Italian school of painting, but there is no Italian school; there were the schools of each city. Every town in Italy, from Venice itself, queen of the sea, to the little hill fortress of Perugia, each had its own school of art, each different and all beautiful.

So do not mind what art Philadelphia or New York is having, but make by the hands of your own citizens beautiful art for the joy of your own citizens, for you have here the primary elements of a great artistic movement.

For, believe me, the conditions of art are much simpler than people imagine. For the noblest art one requires a clear healthy atmosphere, not polluted as the air of our English cities is by the smoke and grime and horridness which comes from open furnace and from factory chimney. You must have strong, sane, healthy physique among your men and women. Sickly or idle or melancholy people do not help much in art. And lastly, you require a sense of individualism about each man and woman, for this is the essence of art – a desire on the part of man to express himself in the noblest way possible. And this is the reason that the grandest art of the world always came from a republic, Athens, Venice, and Florence – there were no kings there and so their art was as noble and simple as sincere. But if you want to know what kind of art the folly of kings will impose on a country look at the decorative art of France under the *grand monarch*, under Louis the Fourteenth; the gaudy gilt furniture writhing under a sense of its own horror and ugliness, with a nymph smirking at every angle and a dragon mouthing on every claw. Unreal and monstrous art this, and fit only for such peri-wigged pomposities as the nobility of France at that time, but not at all fit for you or me. We do not want the rich to possess more beautiful things but the poor to create more beautiful things; for every man is poor who cannot create. Nor shall the art which you and I need be merely a purple robe woven by a slave and thrown over the whitened body of some leprous king to adorn or to conceal the sin of his luxury, but rather still it be the noble and beautiful expression of a people's noble and beautiful life. Art shall be again the most glorious of all the chords through which the spirit of a great nation finds its noblest utterance.

All around you, I said, lie the conditions for a great artistic movement for every great art. Let us think of one of them; a sculptor, for instance.

If a modern sculptor were to come and say, 'Very well, but where can one find subjects for sculpture out of men who wear frock-coats and chimney-pot hats?' I would tell him to go to the docks of a great city and watch the men loading or unloading the stately ships, working at wheel or windlass, hauling at rope or gangway. I have never watched a man do anything useful who has not been graceful at some moment of his labour: it is only the loafer and the idle saunterer who is as useless and uninteresting to the artist as he is to himself. I would ask the sculptor to go with me to any of your schools or universities, to the running ground and gymnasium, to watch the young men start for a race, hurling quoit or club, kneeling to tie their shoes before leaping, stepping from the boat or bending to the oar, and to carve them; and when he was weary of cities I would ask him to come to your fields and meadows to watch the reaper with his sickle and the cattle driver with lifted lasso. For if a man cannot find the noblest motives for his art in such simple daily things as a woman drawing water from the well or a man leaning with his scythe, he will not find them anywhere at all. Gods and goddesses the Greek carved because he loved them; saint and king the Goth because he believed in them. But you, you do not care much for Greek gods and goddesses, and you are perfectly and entirely right; and you do not think much of kings either, and you are quite right. But what you do love are your own men and women, your own flowers and fields, your own hills and mountains, and these are what your art should represent to you.

Ours has been the first movement which has brought the handicraftsman and the artist together, for remember that by separating the one from the other you do ruin to both; you rob the one of all spiritual motive and all imaginative joy, you isolate the other from all real technical perfection. The two greatest schools of art in the world, the sculptor at Athens and the school of painting at Venice, had their origin entirely in a long succession of simple and earnest handicraftsmen. It was the Greek potter who taught the sculptor that restraining influence of design which was the glory of the Parthenon; it was the Italian decorator of chests and household goods who kept Venetian painting always true to its primary pictorial condition of noble colour. For we should remember that all the arts are fine arts and all the arts decorative arts. The greatest triumph of Italian painting was the decoration of a pope's chapel in Rome and the wall of a room in Venice. Michelangelo wrought the one, and Tintoret, the dyer's son, the other. And the little 'Dutch landscape, which you put over your sideboard to-day, and between the windows tomorrow, is' no less a glorious 'piece of work than the extents of field and forest with which Benozzo has made green and beautiful the once melancholy arcade of the Campo Santo at Pisa,' as Ruskin says.

Do not imitate the works of a nation, Greek or Japanese, Italian or English; but their artistic spirit of design and their artistic attitude today, their own world, you should absorb but imitate never, copy never. Unless you can make as beautiful a design in painted china or embroidered screen or beaten brass out of your American turkey as the Japanese does out of his grey silver-winged stork, you will never do anything. Let the Greek carve his lions and the Goth his dragons: buffalo and wild deer are the animals for you.

Golden rod and aster and rose and all the flowers that cover your valleys in the spring and your hills in the autumn: let them be the flowers for your art. Not merely has Nature given you the noblest motives for a new school of decoration, but to you above all other countries has she given the utensils to work in.

You have quarries of marble richer than Pantelicus, more varied than Paros, but do not build a great white square house of marble and think that it is beautiful, or that you are using marble nobly. If you build in marble you must either carve it into joyous decoration, like the lives of dancing children that adorn the marble castles of the Loire, or fill it with beautiful sculpture, frieze and pediment, as the Greeks did, or inlay it with other coloured marbles as they did in Venice. Otherwise you had better build in simple red brick as your Puritan fathers, with no pretence and with some beauty. Do not treat your marble as if it was ordinary stone and build a house of mere blocks of it. For it is indeed a precious stone, this marble of yours, and only workmen of nobility of invention and delicacy of hand should be allowed to touch it at all, carving it into noble statues or into beautiful decoration, or inlaying it with other coloured marbles: for the true colours of architecture are those of natural stone, and I would fain see them taken advantage of to the full. Every variety is here, from pale yellow to purple passing through orange, red and brown, entirely at your command; nearly every kind of green and grey also is attainable, and with these and with pure white what harmony might you not achieve. Of stained and variegated stone the quantity is unlimited, the kinds innumerable. Were brighter colours required, let glass, and gold protected by glass, be used in mosaic, a kind of work as durable as the solid stone and incapable of losing its lustre by time. And let the painter's work be reserved for the shadowed loggia and inner chamber.

This is the true and faithful way of building. Where this cannot be, the device of external colouring may indeed be employed without dishonour – but it must be with the warning reflection that a time will come when such aids will pass away and when the building will be judged in its lifelessness, dying the death of the dolphin. Better the less bright, more enduring fabric. The transparent alabasters of San Miniato and the mosaics of Saint Mark's are more warmly filled and more brightly touched by every return of morning and evening rays, while the hues of the

Gothic cathedrals have died like the iris out of the cloud, and the temples, whose azure and purple once flamed above the Grecian promontory, stand in their faded whiteness like snows which the sunset has left cold.

I do not know anything so perfectly commonplace in design as most modern jewellery. How easy for you to change that and to produce goldsmiths' work that would be a joy to all of us. The gold is ready for you in unexhausted treasure, stored up in the mountain hollow or strewn on the river sand, and was not given to you merely for barren speculation. There should be some better record of it left in your history than the merchant's panic and the ruined home. We do not remember often enough how constantly the history of a great nation will live in and by its art. Only a few thin wreaths of beaten gold remain to tell us of the stately empire of Etruria; and while from the streets of Florence the noble knight and haughty duke have long since passed away, the gates which the simple goldsmith Ghiberti made for their pleasure still guard their lovely house of baptism, worthy still of the praise of Michaelangelo who called them worthy to be the Gates of Paradise.

Have then your school of design, search out your workmen and, when you find one who has delicacy of hand and that wonder of invention necessary for goldsmith's work, do not leave him to toil in obscurity and dishonour and have a great glaring shop and two great glaring shop-boys in it (not to take your orders: they never do that; but to force you to buy something you do not want at all). When you want a thing wrought in gold, goblet or shield for the feast, necklace or wreath for the women, tell him what you like most in decoration, flower or wreath, bird in flight or hound in the chase, image of the woman you love or the friend you honour. Watch him as he beats out the gold into those thin plates delicate as the petals of a yellow rose, or draws it into the long wires like tangled sunbeams at dawn. Whoever that workman be help him, cherish him, and you have such lovely work from his hand as will be a joy to you for all time.

This is the spirit of our movement in England, and this is the spirit in which we would wish you to work, making eternal by your art all that is noble in your men and women, stately in your lakes and mountains, beautiful in your own flowers and natural life. We want to see that you have nothing in your houses that has not been a joy to the man who made it, and is not a joy to those that use it. We want to see you create an art made by the hands of the people to please the hearts of the people too. Do you like this spirit or not? Do you think it simple and strong, noble in its aim, and beautiful in its result? I know you do.

Folly and slander have their own way for a little time, but for a little time only. You now know what we mean: you will be able to estimate what is said of us – its value and its motive.

There should be a law that no ordinary newspaper should be allowed to write about art. The harm they do by their foolish and random writing it would be impossible to overestimate – not to the artist but to the public, blinding them to all, but harming the artist not at all. Without them we would judge a man simply by his work; but at present the newspapers are trying hard to induce the public to judge a sculptor, for instance, never by his statues but by the way he treats his wife; a painter by the amount of his income and a poet by the colour of his necktie. I said there should be a law, but there is really no necessity for a new law: nothing could be easier than to bring the ordinary critic under the head of the criminal classes. But let us leave such an inartistic subject and return to beautiful and comely things, remembering that the art which would represent the spirit of modern newspapers would be exactly the art which you and I want to avoid – grotesque art, malice mocking you from every gateway, slander sneering at you from every corner.

Perhaps you may be surprised at my talking of labour and the workman. You have heard of me, I fear, through the medium of your somewhat imaginative newspapers as, if not a 'Japanese young man', at least a young man to whom the rush and clamour and reality of the modern world were distasteful, and whose greatest difficulty in life was the difficulty of living up to the level of his blue china – a paradox from which England has not yet recovered.

Well, let me tell you how it first came to me at all to create an artistic movement in England, a movement to show the rich what beautiful things they might enjoy and the poor what beautiful things they might create.

One summer afternoon in Oxford – 'that sweet city with her dreaming spires', lovely as Venice in its splendour, noble in its learning as Rome, down the long High Street that winds from tower to tower, past silent cloister and stately gateway, till it reaches that long, grey seven-arched bridge which Saint Mary used to guard (used to, I say, because they are now pulling it down to build a tramway and a light cast-iron bridge in its place, desecrating the loveliest city in England) – well, we were coming down the street – a troop of young men, some of them like myself only nineteen, going to river or tennis-court or cricket-field – when Ruskin going up to lecture in cap and gown met us. He seemed troubled and prayed us to go back with him to his lecture, which a few of us did, and there he spoke to us not on art this time but on life, saying that it seemed to him to be wrong that all the best physique and strength of the young men in England should be spent aimlessly on cricket-ground or river, without any result at all except that if one rowed well one got a pewter pot, and if one made a good score, a cane-handled bat. He thought, he said, that we should be working at something that would do good to other people, at something by which we might show that in all labour there was something noble. Well, we were a good deal moved, and said we would do anything he wished. So he went out round Oxford and found two villages, Upper and Lower Hinksey, and between them there lay a great swamp, so that the villagers could not pass from one to the other without many miles of a round. And when we came back in winter he asked us to help him to make a road across this morass for these village people to use. So out we went, day after day, and learned how to lay levels and to break stones, and to wheel barrows along a plank – a very difficult thing to do. And Ruskin worked with us in the mist and rain and mud of an Oxford winter, and our friends and our enemies came out and mocked us from the bank. We did not mind it much then, and we did not mind it afterwards at all, but worked away for two months at our road. And what became of the road? Well, like a bad lecture it ended abruptly – in the middle of the swamp. Ruskin going away to Venice, when we came back for the next term there was no leader, and the 'diggers', as they called us, fell asunder. And I felt that if there was enough spirit amongst the young men to go out to such work as road-making for the sake of a noble ideal of life, I could from them create an artistic movement that might change, as it has changed, the face of England. So I sought them out – leader they would call me – but there was no leader: we were all searchers only and we were bound to each other by noble friendship and by noble art. There was none of us idle: poets most of us, so ambitious were we: painters some of us, or workers in metal or modellers, determined that we would try and create for ourselves beautiful work: for the handicraftsman beautiful work, for those who love us poems and pictures, for those who love us not epigrams and paradoxes and scorn.

Well, we have done something in England and we will do something more. Now, I do not want you, believe me, to ask your brilliant young men, your beautiful young girls, to go out and make a road on a swamp for any village in America, but I think you might each of you have some art to practise.

We must have, as Emerson said, a mechanical craft for our culture, a basis for our higher accomplishments in the work of our hands – the uselessness of most people's hands seems to me one of the most unpractical things. 'No separation from labour can be without some loss of power or truth to the seer,' says Emerson again. The heroism which would make on us the impression of Epaminondas must be that of a domestic conqueror. The hero of the future is he who shall bravely and gracefully subdue this Gorgon of fashion and of convention.

When you have chosen your own part, abide by it, and do not weakly try and reconcile yourself with the world. The heroic cannot be the common nor the common the heroic. Congratulate yourself if you have done something strange and extravagant and broken the monotony of a decorous age.

And lastly, let us remember that art is the one thing which Death cannot harm. The little house at Concord may be desolate, but the wisdom of New England's Plato is not silenced nor the brilliancy of that Attic genius dimmed: the lips of Longfellow are still musical for us though his dust be turning into the flowers which he loved: and as it is with the greater artists, poet and philosopher and songbird, so let it be with you.

Delivered to the Art students of the Royal Academy at their Club in Golden Square, Westminster, on 30 June 1883. The text is taken from the original manuscript.

Lecture to Art Students

In the lecture which it is my privilege to deliver before you tonight I do not desire to give you any abstract definition of beauty at all. For, we who are working in art cannot accept any theory of beauty in exchange for beauty itself, and, so far from desiring to isolate it in a formula appealing to the intellect, we, on the contrary, seek to materialize it in a form that gives joy to the soul through the senses. We want to create it, not to define it. The definition should follow the work: the work should not adapt itself to the definition.

Nothing, indeed, is more dangerous to the young artist than any conception of ideal beauty: he is constantly led by it either into weak prettiness or lifeless abstraction: whereas to touch the ideal at all you must not strip it of vitality. You must find it in life and re-create it in art.

While, then, on the one hand I do not desire to give you any philosophy of beauty – for, what I want tonight is to investigate how we can create art, not how we can talk of it – on the other hand, I do not wish to deal with anything like a history of English art.

To begin with, such an expression as English art is a meaningless expression. One might just as well talk of English mathematics. Art is the science of beauty, and Mathematics the science of truth: there is no national school of either. Indeed, a national school is a provincial school, merely. Nor is there any such thing as a school of art even. There are merely artists, that is all.

And as regards histories of art, they are quite valueless to you unless you are seeking the ostentatious oblivion of an art professorship. It is of no use to you to know the date of Perugino or the birthplace of Salvator Rosa: all that you should learn about art is to know a good picture when you see it, and a bad picture when you see it. As regards the date of the artist, all good work looks perfectly modern: a piece of Greek sculpture, a portrait of Velazquez – they are always modern, always of our time. And as regards the nationality of the artist, art is not national but universal. As regards archaeology, then, avoid it altogether: archaeology is merely the science of making excuses for bad art; it is the rock on which many a young artist founders and shipwrecks; it is the abyss from which no artist, old or young, ever returns. Or, if he does return, he is so covered with the dust of ages and the mildew of time, that he is quite unrecognizable as an artist, and has to conceal himself for the rest of his days under the cap of a professor, or as a mere illustrator of ancient history. How worthless archaeology is in art you can estimate by the fact of its being so popular. Popularity is the crown of laurel which the world puts on bad art. Whatever is popular is wrong.

As I am not going to talk to you, then, about the philosophy of the beautiful, or the history of art, you will ask me what I am going to talk about. The subject of my lecture tonight is what makes an artist and what does the artist make; what are the relations of the artist to his surroundings, what is the education the artist should get, and what is the quality of a good work of art.

Now, as regards the relations of the artist to his surroundings, by which I mean the age and country in which he is born. All good art, as I said before, has nothing to do with any particular century; but this universality is the quality of the work of art; the conditions that produce that quality are different. And what, I think, you should do is to realize completely your age in order completely to abstract yourself from it; remembering that if you are an artist at all, you will be not the mouthpiece of a century, but the master of eternity; that all art rests on a principle, and that mere temporal considerations are no principle at all; and that those who advise you to make your art representative of the nineteenth century are advising you to produce an art which your children, when you have them, will think old-fashioned. But you will tell me this is an inartistic age, and we are an inartistic people, and the artist suffers much in this nineteenth century of ours.

Of course he does. I, of all men, am not going to deny that. But remember that there never has been an artistic age, or an artistic people, since the beginning of the world. The artist has always been, and will always be, an exquisite exception. There is no golden age of art; only artists who have produced what is more golden than gold.

What, you will say to me, the Greeks? Were not they an artistic people?

Well, the Greeks certainly not, but, perhaps, you mean the Athenians, the citizens of one out of a thousand cities.

Do you think that they were an artistic people? Take them even at the time of their highest artistic development, the latter part of the fifth century before Christ, when they had the greatest poets and the greatest artists of the antique world, when the Parthenon rose in loveliness at the bidding of a Phidias, and the philosopher spake of wisdom in the shadow of the painted portico, and tragedy swept in the perfection of pageant and pathos across the marble of the stage. Were they an artistic people then? Not a bit of it. What is an artistic people but a people who love their artists and understand their art? The Athenians could do neither.

How did they treat Phidias? To Phidias we owe the great era, not merely in Greek, but in all art – I mean of the introduction of the use of the living model.

And what would you say if all the English bishops, backed by the English people, came down from Exeter Hall to the Royal Academy one day and took off Sir Frederick Leighton in a prison van to Newgate on the charge of having allowed you to make use of the living model in your designs for sacred pictures?

Would you not cry out against the barbarism and the Puritanism of such an idea? Would you not explain to them that the worst way to honour God is to dishonour man who is made in His image, and is the work of His hands; and, that if one wants to paint Christ one must take the most Christlike person one can find, and if one wants to paint the Madonna, the purest girl one knows?

Would you not rush off and burn down Newgate, if necessary, and say that such a thing was without parallel in history?

Without parallel? Well, that is exactly what the Athenians did.

In the room of the Parthenon marbles, in the British Museum, you will see a marble shield on the wall. On it there are two figures; one of a man whose face is half hidden, the other of a man with the godlike lineaments of Pericles. For having done this, for having introduced into a bas relief, taken from Greek sacred history, the image of the great statesman who was ruling Athens at the time, Phidias was flung into prison and there, in the common gaol of Athens, died, the supreme artist of the old world.

And do you think that this was an exceptional case? The sign of a Philistine age is the cry of immorality against art, and this cry was raised by the Athenian people against every great poet and thinker of their day – Aeschylus, Euripides, Socrates. It was the same with Florence in the thirteenth century. Good handicrafts are due to guilds not to the people. The moment the guilds lost their power and the people rushed in, beauty and honesty of work died.

And so, never talk of an artistic people; there never has been such a thing.

But, perhaps, you will tell me that the external beauty of the world has almost entirely passed away from us, that the artist dwells no longer in the midst of the lovely surroundings which, in ages past, were the natural inheritance of every one, and that art is very difficult in this unlovely town of ours, where, as you go to your work in the morning, or return from it at eventide, you have to pass through street after street of the most foolish and stupid architecture that the world has ever seen; architecture, where every lovely Greek form is desecrated and defiled, and every lovely Gothic form defiled and desecrated, reducing three-fourths of the London houses to being, merely, like square boxes of the vilest proportions, as gaunt as they are grimy, and as poor as they are pretentious – the hall door always of the wrong colour, and the windows of the wrong size, and where, even when wearied of the houses you turn to contemplate the street itself, you have nothing to look at but chimney-pot hats, men with sandwich boards, vermilion letterboxes, and do that even at the risk of being run over by an emerald-green omnibus.

Is not art difficult, you will say to me, in such surroundings as these? Of course it is difficult, but then art was never easy; you yourselves would not wish it to be easy; and, besides, nothing is worth doing except what the world says is impossible.

Still, you do not care to be answered merely by a paradox. What are the relations of the artist to the external world, and what is the result of the loss of beautiful surroundings to you, is one of the most important questions of modern art; and there is no point on which Mr Ruskin so insists as that the decadence of art has come from the decadence of beautiful things; and that when the artist cannot feed his eye on beauty, beauty goes from his work.

I remember in one of his lectures, after describing the sordid aspect of a great English city, he draws for us a picture of what were the artistic surroundings long ago.

Think, he says, in words of perfect and picturesque imagery, whose beauty I can but feebly echo, think of what was the scene which presented itself, in his afternoon walk, to a designer of the Gothic school of Pisa – Nino Pisano or any of his men[1]:

On each side of a bright river he saw rise a line of brighter palaces, arched and pillared, and inlaid with deep red porphyry, and with serpentine; along the quays before their gates were riding troops of knights, noble in face and form, dazzling in crest and shield; horse and man one labyrinth of quaint colour and gleaming light – the purple, and silver, and scarlet fringes flowing over the strong limbs and clashing mail, like sea-waves over rocks at sunset. Opening on each side from the river were gardens, courts and cloisters; long successions of white pillars among wreaths of vine; leaping of fountains through buds of pomegranate and orange: and still along the garden paths, and under and through the crimson of the pomegranate shadows, moving slowly, groups of the fairest women that Italy ever saw – fairest, because purest and thoughtfullest; trained in all high knowledge, as in all courteous art – in dance, in song, in sweet wit, in lofty learning, in loftier courage, in loftiest love – able alike to cheer, to enchant, or save, the souls of men. Above all this scenery of perfect

[1] *The Two Paths*, Lect. III. p. 123 (1859 ed.).

human life, rose dome and bell-tower, burning with white alabaster and gold: beyond dome and bell-tower the slopes of mighty hills, hoary with olive; far in the north, above a purple sea of peaks of solemn Apennine, the clear, sharp-cloven Carrara mountains sent up their steadfast flames of marble summit into amber sky; the great sea itself, scorching with expanse of light, stretching from their feet to the Gorgonian isles; and over all these, ever present, near or far – seen through the leaves of vine, or imaged with all its march of clouds in the Arno's stream, or set with its depth of blue close against the golden hair and burning check of lady and knight – that untroubled and sacred sky, which was to all men, in those days of innocent faith, indeed the unquestioned abode of spirits, as the earth was of men; and which opened straight through its gates of cloud and veils of dew into the awfulness of the eternal world; a heaven in which every cloud that passed was literally the chariot of an angel, and every ray of its Evening and Morning streamed from the throne of God.

What think you of that for a school of design?

And then look at the depressing, monotonous appearance of any modern city, the sombre dress of men and women, the meaningless and barren architecture, the colourless and dreadful surroundings. Without a beautiful national life, not sculpture merely, but all the arts will die.

Well, as regards the religious feeling of the close of the passage, I do not think I need speak about that. Religion springs from religious feeling, art from artistic feeling: you never get one from the other; unless you have the right root you will not get the right flower; and if a man sees in a cloud the chariot of an angel, he will probably paint it very unlike a cloud.

But, as regards the general idea of the early part of that lovely bit of prose, is it really true that beautiful surroundings are necessary for the artist? I think not; I am sure not. Indeed, to me the most inartistic thing in this age of ours is not the indifference of the public to beautiful things, but the indifference of the artist to the things that are called ugly. For, to the real artist, nothing is beautiful or ugly in itself at all. With the facts of the object he has nothing to do, but with its appearance only, and appearance is a matter of light and shade, of masses, of position, and of value.

Appearance is, in fact, a matter of effect merely, and it is with the effects of nature that you have to deal, not with the real condition of the object. What you, as painters, have to paint is not things as they are but things as they seem to be, not things as they are but things as they are not.

No object is so ugly that, under certain conditions of light and shade, or proximity to other things, it will not look beautiful; no object is so beautiful that, under certain conditions, it will not look ugly. I believe that in every twenty-four hours what is beautiful looks ugly, and what is ugly looks beautiful, once.

And, the commonplace character of so much of our English painting seems to me due to the fact that so many of our young artists look merely at what we may call 'ready-made beauty', whereas you exist as artists not to copy beauty but to create it in your art, to wait and watch for it in nature.

What would you say of a dramatist who would take nobody but virtuous people as characters in his play? Would you not say he was missing half of life? Well, of the young artist who paints nothing but beautiful things, I say he misses one half of the world.

Do not wait for life to be picturesque, but try and see life under picturesque conditions. These conditions you can create for yourself in your studio, for they are merely conditions of light. In nature, you must wait for them, watch for them, choose them; and, if you wait and watch, come they will.

In Gower Street at night you may see a letter-box that is picturesque; on the Thames Embankment you may see picturesque policemen. Even Venice is not always beautiful, nor France.

To paint what you see is a good rule in art, but to see what is worth painting is better. See life under pictorial conditions. It is better to live in a city of changeable weather than in a city of lovely surroundings.

Now, having seen what makes the artist, and what the artist makes, who is the artist? There is a man living amongst us who unites in himself all the qualities of the noblest art, whose work is a joy for all time, who is, himself, a master of all time. That man is Mr Whistler.

*

But, you will say, modern dress, that is bad. If you cannot paint black cloth you could not have painted silken doublet. Ugly dress is better for art – facts of vision, not of the object.

What is a picture? Primarily, a picture is a beautifully coloured surface, merely, with no more spiritual message or meaning for you than an exquisite fragment of Venetian glass or a blue tile from the wall of Damascus. It is, primarily, a purely decorative thing, a delight to look at.

All archaeological pictures that make you say 'How curious!' all sentimental pictures that make you say 'How sad!' all historical pictures that make you say 'How interesting!' all pictures that do not immediately give you such artistic joy as to make you say 'How beautiful!' are bad pictures.

We never know what an artist is going to do. Of course not. The artist is not a specialist. All such divisions as animal painters, landscape painters, painters of Scotch cattle in an English mist, painters of English cattle in a Scotch mist, racehorse painters, bull-terrier painters, all are shallow. If a man is an artist he can paint everything.

The object of art is to stir the most divine and remote of the chords which make music in our soul; and colour is, indeed, of itself a mystical presence on things, and tone a kind of sentinel.

Am I pleading, then, for mere technique? No. As long as there are any signs of technique at all, the picture is unfinished. What is finish? A picture is finished when all traces of work, and of the means employed to bring about the result, have disappeared.

In the case of handicraftsmen – the weaver, the potter, the smith – on their work are the traces of their hand. But it is not so with the painter; it is not so with the artist.

Art should have no sentiment about it but its beauty, no technique except what you cannot observe. One should be able to say of a picture not that it is 'well painted', but that it is 'not painted'.

What is the difference between absolutely decorative art and a painting? Decorative art emphasizes its material: imaginative art annihilates it. Tapestry shows its threads as part of its beauty:

a picture annihilates its canvas; it shows nothing of it. Porcelain emphasizes its glaze: water-colours reject the paper.

A picture has no meaning but its beauty, no message but its joy. That is the first truth about art that you must never lose sight of. A picture is a purely decorative thing.

A 'Jolly' Art Critic

Pall Mall Gazette, 18 November 1886

There is a healthy bank-holiday atmosphere about this book which is extremely pleasant. Mr Quilter is entirely free from affectation of any kind. He rollicks through art with the recklessness of the tourist and describes its beauties with the enthusiasm of the auctioneer. To many, no doubt, he will seem to be somewhat blatant and bumptious, but we prefer to regard him as being simply British. Mr Quilter is the apostle of the middle classes, and we are glad to welcome his gospel. After listening so long to the Don Quixote of art, to listen once to Sancho Panza is both salutary and refreshing.

As for his *Sententiae*, they differ very widely in character and subject. Some of them are ethical, such as 'Humility may be carried too far'; some literary, as 'For one Froude there are a thousand Mrs Markhams'; and some scientific, as 'Objects which are near display more detail than those which are further off.' Some, again, breathe a fine spirit of optimism, as 'Picturesqueness is the birthright of the bargee'; others are jubilant, as 'Paint firm and be jolly'; and many are purely autobiographical, such as No. 97, 'Few of us understand what it is that we mean by Art.' Nor is Mr Quilter's manner less interesting than his matter. He tells us that at this festive season of the year, with Christmas and roast beef looming before us, 'Similes drawn from eating and its results occur most readily to the mind.' So he announces that 'Subject is the diet of painting', that 'Perspective is the bread of art', and that 'Beauty is in some way like jam'; drawings, he points out, 'are not made by recipe like puddings', nor is art composed of 'suet, raisins and candied peel', though Mr Cecil Lawson's landscapes do 'smack of indigestion'. Occasionally, it is true, he makes daring excursions into other realms of fancy, as when the says that 'in the best Reynolds landscapes, one seems *to smell the sawdust*', or that 'advance in art is of a *kangaroo* character'; but, on the whole, he is happiest in his eating similes, and the secret of his style is evidently 'La métaphore vient en mangeant.'

About artists and their work Mr Quilter has, of course, a great deal to say. Sculpture he regards as 'Painting's poor relation'; so, with the exception of a jaunty allusion to the 'rough modelling' of Tanagra figurines he hardly refers at all to the plastic arts; but on painters he writes with much vigour and joviality. Holbein's wonderful Court portraits naturally do not give him much pleasure; in fact, he compares them as works of art to the sham series of Scottish kings at Holyrood; but Doré, he tells us, had a wider imaginative range in all subjects where the gloomy and the terrible played leading parts than probably any artist who ever lived, and may be called 'the Carlyle of artists'. In Gainsborough he sees 'a plainness almost amounting to brutality', while 'vulgarity and snobbishness' are the chief qualities he finds in Sir Joshua Reynolds. He has grave doubts whether Sir Frederick Leighton's work is really 'Greek, after all', and can discover in it but little of 'rocky Ithaca'. Mr Poynter, however, is a carthorse compared to the President, and Frederick Walker was 'a dull Greek' because he had no 'sympathy with poetry'. Linnell's pictures are 'a sort of "Up, Guards, and at 'em" paintings', and Mason's exquisite idylls are 'as national as a Jingo poem'! Mr Birket Foster's landscapes 'smile at one much in the same way that Mr Carker used to "flash his teeth",' and Mr John Collier gives his sitter 'a cheerful slap on the back, before he says, like a shampooer in a Turkish bath, "Next man!"' Mr Herkomer's art is, 'if not a catch-penny art, at all events a catch-many-pounds art', and Mr W. B. Richmond is a 'clever trifler', who 'might do really good work' 'if he would employ his time in learning to paint.' It is obviously unnecessary for us to point out how luminous these criticisms are, how delicate in expression. The remarks on Sir Joshua Reynolds alone exemplify the truth of *Sententia* No. 19, 'From a picture we gain but little more than we bring.' On the general principles of art Mr Quilter writes with equal lucidity. That there is a difference between colour and colours, that an artist, be he portrait-painter or dramatist, always reveals himself in his manner, are ideas that can hardly be said to occur to him; but Mr Quilter really does his best and bravely faces every difficulty in modern art, with the exception of Mr Whistler. Painting, he tells us, is 'of a different quality to mathematics', and finish in art is 'adding more fact'! Portrait painting is a bad pursuit for an emotional artist as it destroys his personality and his sympathy; however, even for the emotional artist there is hope, as a portrait can be converted into a picture 'by adding to the likeness of the sitter some dramatic interest or some picturesque adjunct'! As for etchings, they are of two kinds – British and foreign. The latter fail in 'propriety'. Yet, 'really fine etching is as free and easy as is the chat between old chums at midnight over a smoking-room fire.' Consonant with these rollicking views of art is Mr Quilter's healthy admiration for 'the three primary colours: red, blue and yellow.' Any one, he points out, 'can paint in good tone who paints only in black and white,' and 'the great sign of a good decorator' is 'his capability of doing without neutral tints'. Indeed, on decoration Mr Quilter is almost eloquent. He laments most bitterly the divorce that has been made between decorative art and 'what we usually call "pictures",' makes the customary appeal to the *Last Judgement*, and reminds us that in the great days of art Michelangelo was the 'furnishing upholsterer'. With the present tendencies of decorative art in England Mr Quilter, consequently, has but little sympathy, and he make a gallant appeal to the British householder to stand no more nonsense. Let the honest fellow, he says, on his return from his counting-house tear down the Persian hangings, put a chop on the Anatolian plate, mix some toddy in the Venetian glass, and carry his wife off to the National Gallery to look at 'our own Mulready'! And then the picture he draws of the ideal home, where everything, though ugly, is hallowed by domestic memories, and where beauty appeals not to the heartless eye but the family affections; 'baby's chair there, and the mother's work-basket . . . near the fire, and the ornaments Fred brought home from India on the mantel-board'! It is really impossible not to be touched by so charming a description. How valuable, also, in connection with house decoration is *Sententia* No. 351, 'There is nothing furnishes a room like a bookcase, *and plenty of books in it.*' How cultivated the mind that thus raises literature to the position of upholstery and puts thought on a level with the antimacassar!

And, finally, for the young workers in art Mr Quilter has loud words of encouragement. With a sympathy that is absolutely reckless of grammar, he knows from experience 'what an amount of study and mental strain *are* involved in painting a bad picture honestly'; he exhorts them (*Sententia* No. 267) to 'go on quite bravely and sincerely making mess after mess from Nature,' and while sternly warning them that there is something wrong if they do not 'feel *washed out* after each drawing', he still urges them to 'put a new piece of goods in the window' every morning. In fact, he is quite severe on Mr Ruskin for not recognizing that 'a picture should denote the frailty of man', and remarks with pleasing courtesy and felicitous grace that 'many phases of feeling . . . are as much a dead letter to this great art teacher, as Sanskrit to *an Islington cabman.*' Nor is Mr Quilter one of those who fails to practise what he preaches. Far from it. He goes on quite bravely and sincerely making mess after mess from litera-ture, and misquotes Shakespeare, Wordsworth, Alfred de Musset, Mr Matthew Arnold, Mr Swinburne, and Mr Fitzger-ald's *Rubaiyat*, in strict accordance with *Sententia* No. 251, which tells us that 'Work must be abominable if it is ever going to be good.' Only, unfortunately, his own work never does get good. Not content with his misquotations, he misspells the names of such well-known painters as Madox-Brown, Bastien Lepage and Meissonier, hesitates between Ingrès and Ingres, talks of *Mr* Millais and *Mr* Linton, alludes to Mr Frank Holl simply as 'Hall', speaks with easy familiarity of Mr Burne-Jones as 'Jones', and writes of the artist whom he calls 'old Chrome' with an affection that reminds us of Mr Tulliver's love for Jeremy Taylor. On the whole, the book will not do. We fully admit that it is extremely amusing and, no doubt, Mr Quilter is quite earnest in his endeavours to elevate art to the dignity of manual labour, but the extraordinary vulgarity of the style alone will always be sufficient to prevent these *Sententiae Artis* from being anything more than curiosities of literature. Mr Quilter has missed his chance; for he has failed even to make himself the Tupper of Painting.

Sententiae Artis: First Principles of Art for Painters and Picture Lovers. By Harry Quilter, MA. (Isbister)

The New President

Pall Mall Gazette, 26 January 1889

In a little book that he calls *The Enchanted Island* Mr Wyke Bayliss, the new President of the Royal Society of British Artists, has given his gospel of art to the world. His predecessor in office had also a gospel of art but it usually took the form of an autobiography. Mr Whistler always spelt art, and we believe still spells it, with a capital 'I'. However, he was never dull. His brilliant wit, his caustic satire and his amusing epigrams, or, perhaps, we should say epitaphs, on his contemporaries, made his views on art as delightful as they were misleading and as fascinating as they were unsound. Besides, he introduced American humour into art criticism, and for this, if for no other reason, he deserves to be affectionately remembered. Mr Wyke Bayliss, upon the other hand, is rather tedious. The last President never said much that was true, but the present President never says anything that is new; and, if art be a fairy-haunted wood or an enchanted island, we must say that we prefer the old Puck to the fresh Prospero. Water is an admirable thing – at least, the Greeks said it was – and Mr Ruskin is an admirable writer; but a combination of both is a little depressing.

Still, it is only right to add that Mr Wyke Bayliss, at his best, writes very good English. Mr Whistler, for some reason or other, always adopted the phraseology of the minor prophets. Possibly it was in order to emphasize his well-known claims to verbal inspiration, or perhaps he thought with Voltaire that *Habakkuk était capable de tout*, and wished to shelter himself under the shield of a definitely irresponsible writer none of whose prophecies, according to the French philosopher, has ever been fulfilled. The idea was clever enough at the beginning, but ultimately the manner became monotonous. The spirit of the Hebrews is excellent but their mode of writing is not to be imitated, and no amount of American jokes will give it that modernity which is essential to a good literary style. Admirable as are Mr Whistler's fireworks on canvas, his fireworks in prose are abrupt, violent and exaggerated. However, oracles, since the days of the Pythia, have never been remarkable for style, and the modest Mr Wyke Bayliss is as much Mr Whistler's superior as a writer as he is his inferior as a painter and an artist. Indeed, some of the passages in this book are so charmingly writen and with such felicity of phrase that we cannot help feeling that the President of the British Artists, like a still more famous President of our day, can express himself far better through the medium of litera-ture than he can through the medium of line and colour. This, however, applies only to Mr Wyke Bayliss's prose. His poetry is very bad, and the sonnets at the end of the book are almost as mediocre as the drawings that accompany them. As we read them we cannot but regret that, in this point at any rate, Mr Bayliss has not imitated the wise example of his predecessor who, with all his faults, was never guilty of writing a line of poetry, and is, indeed, quite incapable of doing anything of the kind.

As for the matter of Mr Bayliss's discourses, his views on art must be admitted to be very commonplace and old-fashioned. What is the use of telling artists that they should try and paint Nature as she really is? What Nature really is, is a question for metaphysics not for art. Art deals with appearances, and the eye of the man who looks at Nature, the vision, in fact, of the artist, is far more important to us than what he looks at. There is more truth in Corot's aphorism that a landscape is simply 'the mood of a man's mind' than there is in all Mr Bayliss's laborious disquisitions on naturalism. Again, why does Mr Bayliss waste a whole chapter in pointing out real or supposed resemblances between a book of his published twelve years ago and an article by Mr Palgrave which appeared recently in the *Nineteenth Century*? Neither the book nor the article contains anything of real interest, and as for the hundred or more parallel passages which Mr Wyke Bayliss solemnly prints side by side, most of them are like parallel lines and never meet. The only original proposal that Mr Bayliss has to offer us is that the House of Commons should, every year, select some important event from national and contemporary history and hand it over to the artists who are to choose from among themselves a man to make a picture of it. In this way Mr Bayliss believes that we could have the historic art, and suggests as examples of what he means a picture of Florence Nightingale in the hospital at Scutari, a picture of the opening of the first London Board-school, and a picture of the Senate House at Cambridge with the girl graduate receiving a degree 'that shall acknowledge her to be as wise as Merlin himself and leave her still as beautiful as Vivien.' This proposal is, of course, very well meant, but, to say nothing of the danger of leaving historic art at the mercy of a majority in the House of Commons, who would naturally vote for its own view of things, Mr Bayliss does not seem to realize that a great event is not necessarily a pictorial event. 'The decisive events of the world,' as has been well said, 'take place in the intellect,' and as for Board-schools, academic ceremonies, hospital wards and the like, they may well be left to the artists of the illustrated papers, who do them admirably and quite as well as they need be done. Indeed, the pictures of contemporary events, Royal marriages, naval reviews and things of this kind that appear in the Academy every year, are always extremely bad; while the very same subjects treated in black and white in the *Graphic* or the *London News* are excellent. Besides, if we want to understand the history of a nation through the medium of art, it is to the imaginative and ideal arts that we have to go and not to the arts that are definitely imitative. The visible aspect of life no longer contains for us the secret of life's spirit. Probably it never did contain it. And, if Mr Barker's *Waterloo Banquet* and Mr Frith's *Marriage of the Prince of Wales* are examples of healthy historic art, the less we have of such art the better. However, Mr Bayliss is full of the most ardent faith and speaks quite gravely of genuine portraits of St John, St Peter and St Paul dating from the first century, and of the establishment by the Israelites of a school of art in the wilderness under the now little appreciated Bezaleel. He is a pleasant, picturesque writer, but he should not speak about art. Art is a sealed book to him.

The Enchanted Island. By Wyke Bayliss, FSA, President of the Royal Society of British Artists. (Allen and Co.)

Mr Pater's
Imaginary Portraits

Pall Mall Gazette, 11 June 1887

To convey ideas through the medium of images has always been the aim of those who are artists as well as thinkers in literature, and it is to a desire to give a sensuous environment to intellectual concepts that we owe Mr Pater's last volume. For these Imaginary or, as we should prefer to call them, Imaginative Portraits of his, form a series of philosophic studies in which the philosophy is tempered by personality, and the thought shown under varying conditions of mood and manner, the very permanence of each principle gaining something through the change and colour of the life through which it finds expression. The most fascinating of all these pictures is undoubtedly that of Sebastian Van Storck. The account of Watteau is perhaps a little too fanciful, and the description of him as one who was 'always a seeker after something in the world, that is there is no satisfying measure, or not at all,' seems to us more applicable to him who saw Mona Lisa sitting among the rocks than to the gay and debonair *peintre des fêtes galantes*. But Sebastian, the grave young Dutch philosopher, is charmingly drawn. From the first glimpse we get of him, skating over the water-meadows with his plume of squirrel's tail and his fur muff, in all the modest pleasantness of boyhood, down to his strange death in the desolate house amid the sands of the Helder, we seem to see him, to know him, almost to hear the low music of his voice. He is a dreamer, as the common phrase goes, and yet he is poetical in this sense, that his theorems shape life for him, directly. Early in youth he is stirred by a fine saying of Spinoza, and sets himself to realize the ideal of an intellectual disinterestedness, separating himself more and more from the transient world of sensation, accident and even affection, till what is finite and relative becomes of no interest to him, and he feels that as nature is but a thought of his, so he himself is but a passing thought of God. This conception, of the power of a mere metaphysical abstraction over the mind of one so fortunately endowed for the reception of the sensible world, is exceedingly delightful, and Mr Pater has never written a more subtle psychological study, the fact that Sebastian dies in an attempt to save the life of a little child giving to the whole story a touch of poignant pathos and sad irony.

Denys l'Auxerrois is suggested by a figure found, or said to be found, on some old tapestries in Auxerre, the figure of a 'flaxen and flowery creature, sometimes wellnigh naked among the vine-leaves, sometimes muffled in skins against the cold, sometimes in the dress of a monk, but always with a strong impress of real character and incident from the veritable streets' of the town itself. From this strange design Mr Pater has fashioned a curious mediaeval myth of the return of Dionysus among men, a myth steeped in colour and passion and old romance, full of wonder and full of worship, Denys himself being half animal and half god, making the world mad with a new ecstasy of living, stirring the artists simply by his visible presence, drawing the marvel of music from reed and pipe, and slain at last in a stage-play by those who had loved him. In its rich affluence of imagery this story is like a picture by Mantegna, and indeed Mantegna might have suggested the description of the pageant in which Denys rides upon a gaily painted chariot, in soft silken raiment and, for head-dress, a strange elephant scalp with gilded tusks.

If *Denys l'Auxerrois* symbolizes the passion of the senses and *Sebastian Van Storck* the philosophic passion, as they certainly seem to do, though no mere formula or definition can adequately express the freedom and variety of the life that they portray, the passion for the imaginative world of art is the basis of the story of *Duke Carl of Rosenmold*. Duke Carl is not unlike the late King of Bavaria, in his love of France, his admiration for the *Grand Monarque* and his fantastic desire to amaze and to bewilder, but the resemblance is possibly only a chance one. In fact Mr Pater's young hero is the precursor of the *Aufklärung* of the last century, the German precursor of Herder and Lessing and Goethe himself, and finds the forms of art ready to his hand without any national spirit to fill them or make them vital and responsive. He too dies, trampled to death by the soldiers of the country he so much admired, on the night of his marriage with a peasant girl, the very failure of his life lending him a certain melancholy grace and dramatic interest.

On the whole, then, this is a singularly attractive book. Mr Pater is an intellectual impressionist. He does not weary us with any definite doctrine or seek to suit life to any formal creed. He is always looking for exquisite moments and, when he has found them, he analyses them with delicate and delightful art and then passes on, often to the opposite pole of thought or feeling, know-ing that every mood has its own quality and charm and is justified by its mere existence. He has taken the sensationalism of Greek philosophy and made it a new method of art criticism. As for his style, it is curiously ascetic. Now and then, we come across phrases with a strange sensuousness of expression, as when he tells us how Denys l'Auxerrois, on his return from a long journey, 'ate flesh for the first time, tearing the hot, red morsels with his delicate fingers in a kind of wild greed,' but such passages are rare. Asceticism is the keynote of Mr Pater's prose; at times it is almost too severe in its self-control and makes us long for a little more freedom. For indeed, the danger of such prose as his is that it is apt to become somewhat laborious. Here and there, one is tempted to say of Mr Pater that he is 'a seeker after something in language, that is there in no satisfying measure, or not at all.' The continual preoccupation with phrase and epithet has its drawbacks as well as its virtues. And yet, when all is said, what wonderful prose it is, with its subtle preferences, its fastidious purity, its rejection of what is common or ordinary! Mr Pater has the true spirit of selection, the true tact of omission. If he be not among the greatest prose writers of our literature he is, at least, our greatest artist in prose; and though it may be admitted that the best style is that which seems an unconcious result rather than a conscious aim, still in these latter days when violent rhetoric does duty for eloquence and vulgarity usurps the name of nature, we should be grateful for a style that deliberately aims at perfection of form, that seeks to produce its effect by artistic means and sets before itself an ideal of grave and chastened beauty.

Imaginary Portraits. By Walter Pater, MA, Fellow of Brasenose College, Oxford. (Macmillan and Co.)

Mr Pater's Appreciations

Speaker, 22 March 1890

W hen I first had the privilege – and I count it a very high
one – of meeting Mr Walter Pater, he said to me, smiling,
'Why do you always write poetry? Why do you not write prose?
Prose is so much more difficult.'

It was during my undergraduate days at Oxford; days of
lyrical ardour and of studious sonnet-writing; days when one
loved the exquisite intricacy and musical repetitions of the ballade, and the villanelle with its linked long-drawn echoes and its
curious completeness; days when one solemnly sought to discover
the proper temper in which a triolet should be written; delightful
days, in which, I am glad to say, there was far more rhyme than
reason.

I may frankly confess now that at the time I did not quite
comprehend what Mr Pater really meant; and it was not till I
had carefully studied his beautiful and suggestive essays on the
Renaissance that I fully realized what a wonderful self-conscious
art the art of English prose-writing really is, or may be made to
be. Carlyle's stormy rhetoric, Ruskin's winged and passionate
eloquence, had seemed to me to spring from enthusiasm rather
than from art. I do not think I knew then that even prophets
correct their proofs. As for Jacobean prose, I thought it too
exuberant; and Queen Anne prose appeared to me terribly bald,
and irritatingly rational. But Mr Pater's essays became to me
'the golden book of spirit and sense, the holy writ of beauty'.
They are still this to me. It is possible, of course, that I may
exaggerate about them. I certainly hope that I do; for where
there is no exaggeration there is no love, and where there is no
love there is no understanding. It is only about things that do
not interest one, that one can give a really unbiased opinion;

and this is no doubt the reason why an unbiased opinion is always valueless.

But I must not allow this brief notice of Mr Pater's new volume to degenerate into an autobiography. I remember being told in America that whenever Margaret Fuller wrote an essay upon Emerson the printers had always to send out to borrow some additional capital 'I's', and I feel it right to accept this transatlantic warning.

Appreciations, in the fine Latin sense of the word, is the title given by Mr Pater to his book, which is an exquisite collection of exquisite essays, of delicately wrought works of art – some of them being almost Greek in their purity of outline and perfection of form, others mediaeval in their strangeness of colour and passionate suggestion, and all of them absolutely modern, in the true meaning of the term modernity. For he to whom the present is the only thing that is present, knows nothing of the age in which he lives. To realize the nineteenth century one must realize every century that has preceded it, and that has contributed to its making. To know anything about oneself, one must know all about others. There must be no mood with which one cannot sympathize, no dead mode of life that one cannot make alive. The legacies of heredity may make us alter our views of moral responsibility, but they cannot but intensify our sense of the value of Criticism; for the true critic is he who bears within himself the dreams and ideas and feelings of myriad generations, and to whom no form of thought is alien, no emotional impulse obscure.

Perhaps the most interesting, and certainly the least successful, of the essays contained in the present volume is that on *Style*. It is the most interesting because it is the work of one who speaks with the high authority that comes from the noble realization of things nobly conceived. It is the least successful, because the subject is too abstract. A true artist like Mr Pater is most felicitous when he deals with the concrete, whose very limitations give him finer freedom, while they necessitate more intense vision. And yet what a high ideal is contained in these few pages! How good it is for us, in these days of popular education and facile journalism, to be reminded of the real scholarship that is essential to the perfect writer, who, 'being a true lover of words for their own sake, a minute and constant observer of their physiognomy,' will avoid what is mere rhetoric, or ostentatious ornament, or negligent misuse of terms, or ineffective surplusage, and will be known by his tact of omission, by his skilful economy of means, by his selection and self-restraint, and perhaps above all by that conscious artistic structure which is the expression of mind in style. I think I have been wrong in saying that the subject is too abstract. In Mr Pater's hands it becomes very real to us indeed, and he shows us how, behind the perfection of a man's style, must lie the passion of a man's soul.

As one passes to the rest of the volume, one finds essays on Wordsworth and on Coleridge, on Charles Lamb and on Sir Thomas Browne, on some of Shakespeare's plays and on the English kings that Shakespeare fashioned, on Dante Rossetti and on William Morris. As that on Wordsworth seems to be Mr Pater's last work, so that on the singer of the *Defence of Guenevere* is certainly his earliest, or almost his earliest, and it is interesting to mark the change that has taken place in his style. This change is, perhaps, at first sight not very apparent. In 1868 we find Mr Pater writing with the same exquisite care for words, with the same studied music, with the same temper, and something of the same mode of treatment. But, as he goes on, the architecture of the style becomes richer and more complex, the epithet more precise and intellectual. Occasionally one may be inclined to think that there is, here and there, a sentence which is somewhat long, and possibly, if one may venture to say so, a little heavy and cumbersome in movement. But if this be so, it comes from those side-issues suddenly suggested by the idea in its progress, and really revealing the idea more perfectly; or from those felicitous afterthoughts that give a fuller completeness to the central scheme, and yet convey something of the charm of chance; or from a desire to suggest the secondary shades of meaning with all their accumulating effect, and to avoid, it may be, the violence and harshness of too definite and exclusive an opinion. For in matters of art, at any rate, thought is inevitably coloured by emotion, and so is fluid rather than fixed, and, recognizing its dependence upon moods and upon the passion of fine moments, will not accept the rigidity of a scientific formula or a theological dogma. The critical pleasure, too, that we receive from tracing, through what may seem the intricacies of a sentence, the working of the constructive intelligence, must not be overlooked. As soon as we have realized the design, everything appears clear and simple. After a time, these long sentences of Mr Pater's come to have the charm of an elaborate piece of music, and the unity of such music also.

I have suggested that the essay on Wordsworth is probably the most recent bit of work contained in this volume. If one might choose between so much that is good, I should be inclined to say it is the finest also. The essay on Lamb is curiously suggestive; suggestive, indeed, of a somewhat more tragic, more sombre figure, than men have been wont to think of in connection with the author of the *Essays of Elia*. It is an interesting aspect under which to regard Lamb, but perhaps he himself would have had some difficulty in recognizing the portrait given of him. He had, undoubtedly, great sorrows, or motives for sorrow, but he could console himself at a moment's notice for the real tragedies of life by reading any one of the Elizabethan tragedies, provided it was in a folio edition. The essay on Sir Thomas Browne is delightful, and has the strange, personal, fanciful charm of the author of the *Religio Medici*, Mr Pater often catching the colour and accent and tone of whatever artist, or work of art, he deals with. That on Coleridge, with its insistence on the necessity of the cultivation of the relative, as opposed to the absolute spirit in philosophy and in ethics, and its high appreciation of the poet's true position in our literature, is in style and substance a very blameless work. Grace of expression and delicate subtlety of thought and phrase, characterize the essays on Shakespeare. But the essay on Wordsworth has a spiritual beauty of its own. It appeals, not to the ordinary Wordsworthian with his uncritical temper, and his gross confusion of ethical and aesthetical problems, but rather to those who desire to separate the gold from the dross, and to reach at the true Wordsworth through the mass of tedious and prosaic work that bears his name, and that serves often to conceal him from us. The presence of an alien element in Wordsworth's art is, of course, recognized by Mr Pater, but he touches on it merely from the psychological point of view, pointing out how this quality of higher and lower moods gives the effect in his poetry 'of a power not altogether his own, or under his control'; a power which comes and goes when it wills, 'so that the old fancy which made the poet's art an enthusiasm, a form of divine possession, seems almost true of him.' Mr Pater's earlier essays had their *purpurei panni*, so eminently suitable for quotation, such as the famous passage on *Mona Lisa*, and that other in which Botticelli's strange conception of the Virgin is so strangely set forth. From the present volume it is difficult to select any one passage in preference to another as specially characteristic of Mr Pater's treatment. This, however, is worth quoting at length. It contains a truth eminently suitable for our age:

That the end of life is not action but contemplation – *being* as distinct from *doing* – a certain disposition of the mind: is, in some shape or other, the principle of all the higher morality. In poetry, in art, if you enter into their true spirit at all, you touch this principle in a measure; these, by their sterility, are a type of beholding for the mere joy of beholding. To treat life in the spirit of art is to make life a thing in which means and ends are identified: to encourage such treatment, the true moral significance of art and poetry. Wordsworth, and other poets who have been like him in ancient or more recent times, are the masters, the experts, in this art of impassioned contemplation. Their work is not to teach lessons, or enforce rules, or even to stimulate us to noble ends, but to withdraw the thoughts for a while from the mere machinery of life, to fix them, with appropriate emotions, on the spectacle of those great facts in man's existence which no machinery affects, 'on the great and universal passions of men, the most general and interesting of their occupations, and the entire world of nature' – on 'the operations of the elements and the appearances of the visible universe, on storm and sunshine, on the revolutions of the seasons, on cold and heat, on loss of friends and kindred, on injuries and resentments, on gratitude and hope, on fear and sorrow.' To witness this spectacle with appropriate emotions is the aim of all culture; and of these emotions poetry like Wordsworth's is a great nourisher and stimulant. He sees nature full of sentiment and excitement; he sees men and women as parts of nature, passionate, excited, in strange grouping and connection with the grandeur and beauty of the natural world – images, in his own words, 'of men suffering, amid awful forms and powers'.

Certainly the real secret of Wordsworth has never been better expressed. After having read and reread Mr Pater's essay – for it requires rereading – one returns to the poet's work with a new sense of joy and wonder, and with something of eager and impassioned expectation. And perhaps this might be roughly taken as the test or touchstone of the finest criticism.

Finally, one cannot help noticing the delicate instinct that has gone to fashion the brief epilogue that ends this delightful volume. The difference between the classical and romantic spirits in art has often, and with much overemphasis, been discussed. But with what a light sure touch does Mr Pater write of it! How subtle and certain are his distinctions! If imaginative prose be really the special art of this century, Mr Pater must rank amongst our century's most characteristic artists. In certain things he stands almost alone. The age has produced wonderful prose styles, turbid with individualism, and violent with excess of rhetoric. But in Mr Pater, as in Cardinal Newman, we find the union of personality with perfection. He has no rival in his own sphere, and he has escaped disciples. And this, not because he has not been imitated, but because in art so fine as his there is something that, in its essence, is inimitable.

Appreciations, with an Essay on Style. By Walter Pater, Fellow of Brasenose College. (Macmillan and Co.)

Some Literary Notes

Woman's World, February 1889

'The various collectors of Irish folk-lore,' says Mr W. B. Yeats in his charming little book *Fairy and Folk Tales of the Irish Peasantry*, 'have, from our point of view, one great merit, and from the point of view of others, one great fault.'

They have made their work literature rather than science, and told us of the Irish peasantry rather than of the primitive religion of mankind, or whatever else the folklorists are on the gad after. To be considered scientists they should have tabulated all their tales in forms like grocers' bills – item the fairy king, item the queen. Instead of this they have caught the very voice of the people, the very pulse of life, each giving what was most noticed in his day. Croker and Lover, full of the ideas of harum-scarum Irish gentility, saw everything humorized. The impulse of the Irish literature of their time came from a class that did not – mainly for political reasons – take the populace seriously, and imagined the country as a humorist's Arcadia; its passion, its gloom, its tragedy, they knew nothing of. What they did was not wholly false; they merely magnified an irresponsible type, found oftenest among boatmen, carmen and gentlemen's servants, into the type of a whole nation, and created the stage Irishman. The writers of 'Forty-eight, and the famine combined, burst their bubble. Their work had the dash as well as the shallowness of an ascendant and idle class, and in Croker is touched everywhere with beauty – a gentle Arcadian beauty. Carleton, a peasant born, has in many of his stories, . . . more especially in his ghost stories, a much more serious way with him, for all his humour. Kennedy, an old bookseller in Dublin, who seems to have had a something of genuine belief in the fairies, comes next in time. He has far less literary faculty, but is wonderfully accurate, giving often the very words the stories were told in. But the best book since Croker is Lady Wilde's *Ancient Legends*. The humour has all given way to pathos and tenderness. We have here the innermost heart of the Celt in the moments he has grown to love through years of persecution, when, cushioning himself about with dreams, and hearing fairy-songs in the twilight, he ponders on the soul and on the dead. Here is the Celt, only it is the Celt dreaming.

Into a volume of very moderate dimensions, and of extremely moderate price, Mr Yeats has collected together the most characteristic of our Irish folklore stories, grouping them together according to subject. First come *The Trooping Fairies*. The peasants say that these are 'fallen angels who were not good enough to be saved, nor bad enough to be lost'; but the Irish antiquarians see in them 'the gods of pagan Ireland', who, 'when no longer worshipped and fed with offerings, dwindled away in the popular imagination, and now are only a few spans high.' Their chief occupations are feasting, fighting, making love, and playing the most beautiful music. 'They have only one industrious person amongst them, the *lepra-caun* – the shoemaker.' It is his duty to repair their shoes when they wear them out with dancing. Mr Yeats tells us that 'near the village of Ballisodare is a little woman who lived amongst them seven years. When she came home she had no toes – she had danced them off.' On May Eve, every seventh year, they fight for the harvest, for the best ears of grain belong to them. An old man informed Mr Yeats that he saw them fight once, and that they tore the thatch off a house. 'Had any one else been near they would merely have seen a great wind whirling everything into the air as it passed.' When the wind drives the leaves and straws before it, 'that is the fairies, and the peasants take off their hats and say "God bless them".' When they are gay, they sing. Many of the most beautiful tunes of Ireland 'are only their music, caught up by eavesdroppers.' No prudent peasant would hum *The Pretty Girl Milking the Cow* near a fairy rath, 'for they are jealous, and do not like to hear their songs on clumsy mortal lips.' Blake once saw a fairy's funeral. But this, as Mr Yeats points out, must have been an English fairy, for the Irish fairies never die; they are immortal.

Then come *The Solitary Fairies*, amongst whom we find the little *Lepracaun* mentioned above. He has grown very rich, as he possesses all the treasure-crocks buried in wartime. In the early part of this century, according to Croker, they used to show in Tipperary a little shoe forgotten by the fairy shoemaker. Then there are two rather disreputable little fairies – the *Cluricaun*, who gets intoxicated in gentlemen's cellars, and the Red Man, who plays unkind practical jokes. 'The *Fear-Gorta* (Man of Hunger) is an emaciated phantom that goes through the land in famine time, begging an alm and bringing good luck to the giver.' The *Water-sheerie* is 'own brother to the English Jack-o'-Lantern'. '*The Leanhaun Shee* (fairy mistress) seeks the love of mortals. If they refuse, she must be their slave; if they consent, they are hers, and can only escape by finding another to take their place. The fairy lives on their life, and they waste away. Death is no escape from her. She is the Gaelic muse, for she gives inspiration to those she persecutes. The Gaelic poets die young, for she is restless, and will not let them remain long on earth.' The *Pooka* is essentially an animal spirit, and some have considered him the forefather of Sheakespeare's 'Puck'. He lives on solitary mountains, and among old ruins 'grown monstrous with much solitude', and 'is of the race of the nightmare'. 'He has many shapes – is now a horse . . . now a goat, now an eagle. Like all spirits, he is only half in the world of form.' The *banshee* does not care much for our democratic levelling tendencies; she loves only old families, and despises the *parvenu* or the *nouveau riche*. When more than one banshee is present, and they wail and sing in chorus, it is for the death of some holy or great one. An omen that sometimes accompanies the banshee is ' . . . an immense black coach, mounted by a coffin, and drawn by headless horses driven by a *Dullahan*.' A *Dullahan* is the most terrible thing in the world. In 1807 two of the sentries stationed outside St James's Park saw one climbing the railings, and died of fright. Mr Yeats suggests that they are possibly 'descended from that Irish giant who swam across the Channel with his head in his teeth.'

Then come the stories of ghosts, of saints and priests, and of giants. The ghosts live in a state intermediary between this world and the next. They are held there by some earthly longing or affection, or some duty unfulfilled, or anger against the living; they are those who are too good for hell, and too bad for heaven. Sometimes they 'take the forms of insects, especially of butterflies'. The author of the *Parochial Survey of Ireland* 'heard a woman say to a child who was chasing a butterfly, "How do you know it is not the soul of your grandfather?" On November eve they are abroad, and dance with the fairies.' As for the saints and priests, 'there are no martyrs in the stories.' That ancient chronicler Giraldus Cambrensis 'taunted the Archbishop of Cashel, because no one in Ireland had received the crown of martyrdom. 'Our people may be barbarous,' the prelate answered, 'but they have never lifted their hands against God's saints; but now that a people have come amongst us who know how to make them (it was just after the English invasion), we shall have martyrs plentifully.'" The giants were the old pagan heroes of Ireland, who grew bigger and bigger, just as the gods grew smaller and smaller. The fact is they did not wait for offerings; they took them *vi et armis*.

Some of the prettiest stories are those that cluster round *Tir-na-n-Og*. This is the Country of the Young, 'for age and death have not found it; neither tears nor loud laughter have gone near it.' 'One man has gone there and returned. The bard, Oisin, who wandered away on a white horse, moving on the surface of the foam with his fairy Niamh, lived there three hundred years, and then returned looking for his comrades. The moment his foot touched the earth his three hundred years fell on him, and he was bowed double, and his beard swept the ground. He described his sojourn in the Land of Youth to Patrick before he died.' Since then, according to Mr Yeats, 'many have seen it in many places; some in the depths of lakes, and have heard rising therefrom a vague sound of bells; more have seen it far off on the horizon, as they peered out from the western cliffs. Not three years ago a fisherman imagined that he saw it.'

Mr Yeats has certainly done his work very well. He has shown great critical capacity in his selection of the stories, and his little introductions are charmingly written. It is delightful to come across a collection of purely imaginative work, and Mr Yeats has a very quick instinct in finding out the best and the most beautiful things in Irish folklore. I am also glad to see that he has not confined himself entirely to prose, but has included Allingham's lovely poem on *The Fairies*:

Up the airy mountain,
    Down the rushy glen,
We daren't go a-hunting
    For fear of little men;
Wee folk, good folk,
    Trooping all together;
Green jacket, red cap,
    And white owl's feather!

Down along the rocky shore
    Some make their home,
They live on crispy pancakes
    Of yellow tide-foam;
Some in the reeds
    Of the black mountain lake,
With frogs for their watch-dogs
    All night awake.

High on the hill-top
    The old King sits;
He is now so old and gray
    He's nigh lost his wits.
With a bridge of white mist
    Columbkill he crosses,
On his stately journeys
    From Slieveleague to Rosses;
Or going up with music,
    On cold starry nights,
To sup with the Queen
    Of the gay Northern Lights.

All lovers of fairy tales and folklore should get this little book. *The Horned Women, The Priest's Soul*[1] and *Teig O'Kane*, are really marvellous in their way; and, indeed, there is hardly a single story that is not worth reading and thinking over.

Fairy and Folk Tales of the Irish Peasantry Edited and selected by W. B. Yeats. (Walter Scott)

[1] From Lady Wilde's *Ancient Legends of Ireland*.

Further Literary Notes

Woman's World, March 1889

*T*he *Wanderings of Oisin and Other Poems* is from the clever pen of Mr W. B. Yeats, whose charming anthology of Irish fairy tales I had occasion to notice in a recent number of the *Woman's World*. It is, I believe, the first volume of poems that Mr Yeats has published, and it is certainly full of promise. It must be admitted that many of the poems are too fragmentary, too incomplete. They read like stray scenes out of unfinished plays, like things only half remembered, or, at best, but dimly seen. But the architectonic power of construction, the power to build up and make perfect a harmonious whole, is nearly always the latest, as it certainly is the highest, development of the artistic temperament. It is somewhat unfair to expect it in early work. One quality Mr Yeats has in a marked degree, a quality that is not common in the work of our minor poets, and is therefore all the more welcome to us – I mean the romantic temper. He is essentially Celtic, and his verse, at its best, is Celtic also. Strongly influenced by Keats, he seems to study how to 'load every rift with ore', yet is more fascinated by the beauty of words than by the beauty of metrical music. The spirit that dominates the whole book is perhaps more valuable than any individual poem or particular passage, but this from *The Wanderings of Oisin* is worth quoting. It describes the ride to the Island of Forgetfulness:

And the ears of the horse went sinking away in the hollow light,
For, as drift from a sailor slow drowning the gleams of the world
and the sun,
Ceased on our hands and faces, on hazel and oak leaf, the light,
And the stars were blotted above us, and the whole of the world
was one;

Till the horse gave a whinny; for cumbrous with stems of the hazel
    and oak,
  Of hollies, and hazels, and oak-trees, a valley was sloping away
From his hoofs in the heavy grasses, with monstrous slumbering folk,
  Their mighty and naked and gleaming bodies heaped loose where
    they lay.

More comely than man may make them, inlaid with silver and gold,
  Were arrow and shield and war-axe, arrow and spear and blade,
And dew-blanched horns, in whose hollows a child of three years old
  Could sleep on a couch of rushes, round and about them laid.

And this, which deals with the old legend of the city lying under
the waters of a lake, is strange and interesting:

The maker of the stars and worlds
  Sat underneath the market cross,
And the old men were walking, walking,
  And little boys played pitch-and-toss.

'The props,' said He, 'of stars and worlds
  Are prayers of patient men and good.'
The boys, the women, and old men,
  Listening, upon their shadows stood.

A grey professor passing cried,
  'How few the mind's intemperance rule!
What shallow thoughts about deep things!
  The world grows old and plays the fool.'

The mayor came, leaning his left ear –
  There were some talking of the poor –
And to himself cried, 'Communist!'
  And hurried to the guardhouse door.

The bishop came with open book,
  Whispering along the sunny path;
There was some talking of man's God,
  His God of stupor and of wrath.

The bishop murmured, 'Atheist!
  How sinfully the wicked scoff!'
And sent the old men on their way,
  And drove the boys and women off.

The place was empty now of people;
  A cock came by upon his toes;
An old horse looked across the fence,
  And rubbed along the rail his nose.

The maker of the stars and worlds
  To His own house did Him betake,
And on that city dropped a tear,
  And now that city is a lake.

Mr Yeats has a great deal of invention, and some of the poems in his book, such as *Mosada*, *Jealousy*, and *The Island of Statues*, are very finely conceived. It is impossible to doubt, after reading his present volume, that he will some day give us work of high import. Up to this he has been merely trying the strings of his instrument, running over the keys.

The Wanderings of Oisin and Other Poems. By W. B. Yeats. (Kegan Paul)

Ben Jonson

Pall Mall Gazette, 20 September 1886

In selecting Mr John Addington Symonds to write the life of
Ben Jonson for his series of 'English Worthies', Mr Lang, no
doubt, exercised a wise judgement. Mr Symonds, like the author
of *Volpone*, is a scholar and a man of letters; his book on *Shakespeare's Predecessors* showed a marvellous knowledge of the Elizabethan period, and he is a recognized authority on the Italian
Renaissance. The last is not the least of his qualifications. Without a full appreciation of the meaning of the Humanistic movement it is impossible to understand the great struggle between
the Classical form and the Romantic spirit which is the chief
critical characteristic of the golden age of the English drama, an
age when Shakespeare found his chief adversary, not among his
contemporaries, but in Seneca, and when Jonson armed himself
with Aristotle to win the suffrages of a London audience. Mr
Symonds' book, consequently, will be opened with interest. It
does not, of course, contain much that is new about Jonson's
life. But the facts of Jonson's life are already well known, and in
books of this kind what is true is of more importance than what
is new, appreciation more valuable than discovery. Scotchmen,
however, will, no doubt, be interested to find that Mr Symonds
has succeeded in identifying Jonson's crest with that of the John-
stones of Annandale, and the story of the way the literary Titan
escaped from hanging, by proving that he could read, is graphi-
cally told.

On the whole, we have a vivid picture of the man as he lived.
Where picturesqueness is required, Mr Symonds is always good.
The usual comparison with Dr Johnson is, of course, brought
out. Few of 'Rare Ben's' biographers spare us that, and the point
is possibly a natural one to make. But when Mr Symonds calls

upon us to notice that both men made a journey to Scotland, and that 'each found in a Scotchman his biographer', the parallel loses all value. There is an M in Monmouth and an M in Macedon, and Drummond of Hawthornden and Boswell of Auchinleck were both born the other side of the Tweed; but from such analogies nothing is to be learned. There is no surer way of destroying a similarity than to strain it.

As for Mr Symonds' estimate of Jonson's genius, it is in many points quite excellent. He ranks him with the giants rather than with the gods, with those who compel our admiration by their untiring energy and huge strength of intellectual muscle, not with those 'who share the divine gifts of creative imagination and inevitable instinct.' Here he is right. Pelion more than Parnassus was Jonson's home. His art has too much effort about it, too much definite intention. His style lacks the charm of chance. Mr Symonds is right also in the stress he lays on the extraordinary combination in Jonson's work of the most concentrated realism with encyclopaedic erudition. In Jonson's comedies London slang and learned scholarship go hand in hand. Literature was as living a thing to him as life itself. He used his classical lore not merely to give form to his verse, but to give flesh and blood to the persons of his plays. He could build up a breathing creature out of quotations. He made the poets of Greece and Rome terribly modern, and introduced them to the oddest company. His very culture is an element in his coarseness. There are moments when one is tempted to liken him to a beast that has fed off books.

We cannot, however, agree with Mr Symonds when he says that Jonson 'rarely touched more than the outside of character', that his men and women are 'the incarnations of abstract properties rather than living human beings', that they are in fact mere 'masqueraders and mechanical puppets'. Eloquence is a beautiful thing but rhetoric ruins many a critic, and Mr Symonds is essentially rhetorical. When, for instance, he tells us that 'Jonson made masks', while 'Dekker and Heywood created souls', we feel that he is asking us to accept a crude judgement for the sake of a smart antithesis. It is, of course, true that we do not find in Jonson the same growth of character that we find in Shakespeare, and we may admit that most of the characters in Jonson's plays are, so to speak, ready-made. But a ready-made character is not necessarily either mechanical or wooden, two epithets Mr Symonds uses constantly in his criticism.

We cannot tell, and Shakespeare himself does not tell us, why Iago is evil, why Regan and Goneril have hard hearts, or why Sir Andrew Aguecheek is a fool. It is sufficient that they are what they are, and that nature gives warrant for their existence. If a character in a play is lifelike, if we recognize it as true to nature, we have no right to insist on the author explaining its genesis to us. We must accept it as it is: and in the hands of a good dramatist mere presentation can take the place of analysis, and indeed is often a more dramatic method, because a more direct one. And Jonson's characters are true to nature. They are in no sense abstractions; they are types. Captain Bobadil and Captain Tucca. Sir John Daw and Sir Amorous La Foole, Volpone and Mosca, Subtle and Sir Epicure Mammon, Mrs Purecraft and the Rabbi Busy are all creatures of flesh and blood, none the less lifelike because they are labelled. In this point Mr Symonds seems to us unjust towards Jonson.

We think, also, that a special chapter might have been devoted to Jonson as a literary critic. The creative activity of the English Renaissance is so great that its achievements in the sphere of criticism are often overlooked by the student. Then, for the first time, was language treated as an art. The laws of expression and composition were investigated and formularized. The importance of words was recognized. Romanticism, Realism and Classicism fought their first battles. The dramatists are full of literary and art criticisms, and amused the public with slashing articles on one another in the form of plays.

Mr Symonds, of course, deals with Jonson in his capacity as a critic, and always with just appreciation, but the whole subject is one that deserves fuller and more special treatment.

Some small inaccuracies, too, should be corrected in the second edition. Dryden, for instance, was not 'Jonson's successor on the laureate's throne', as Mr Symonds eloquently puts it, for Sir William Davenant came between them, and when one remembers the predominance of rhyme in Shakespeare's early plays, it is too much to say that 'after the production of the first part of *Tamburlaine* blank verse became the regular dramatic metre of the public stage.' Shakespeare did not accept blank verse at once as a gift from Marlowe's hand, but himself arrived at it after a long course of experiments in rhyme. Indeed, some of Mr Symonds' remarks on Marlowe are very curious. To say of his *Edward II*, for instance, that it 'is not at all inferior to the work of Shakespeare's younger age,' is very niggardly and inadequate praise, and comes strangely from one who has elsewhere written with such appreciation of Marlowe's great genius; while to call Marlowe Jonson's 'master' is to make for him an impossible claim. In comedy Marlowe has nothing whatever to teach Jonson; in tragedy Jonson sought for the classical not the romantic form.

As for Mr Symonds' style, it is, as usual, very fluent, very picturesque and very full of colour. Here and there, however, it is really irritating. Such a sentence as 'the tavern had the defects of its quality' is an awkward Gallicism; and when Mr Symonds, after genially comparing Jonson's blank verse to the front of Whitehall (a comparison, by the way, that would have enraged the poet beyond measure) proceeds to play a fantastic aria on the same string, and tells us that 'Massinger reminds us of the intricacies of Sansovino, Shakespeare of Gothic aisles or heaven's cathedral . . . Ford of glittering Corinthian colonnades, Webster of vaulted crypts, . . . Marlowe of masoned clouds, and Marston, in his better moments, of the fragmentary vigour of a Roman ruin,' one begins to regret that any one ever thought of the unity of the arts. Similes such as these obscure; they do not illumine. To say that Ford is like a glittering Corinthian colonnade adds nothing to our knowledge of either Ford or Greek architecture. Mr Symonds has written some charming poetry, but his prose, unfortunately, is always poetical prose, never the prose of a poet. Still, the volume is worth reading, though decidedly Mr Symonds, to use one of his own phrases, has 'the defects of his quality'.

'English Worthies.' Edited by Andrew Lang. *Ben Jonson*. By John Addington Symonds. (Longmans, Green and Co.)

Balzac in English

Pall Mall Gazette, 13 September 1886

Many years ago, in a number of *All the Year Round*, Charles Dickens complained that Balzac was very little read in England, and although since then the public has become more familiar with the great masterpieces of French fiction, still it may be doubted whether the *Comédie Humaine* is at all appreciated or understood by the general run of novel readers. It is really the greatest monument that literature has produced in our century, and M. Taine hardly exaggerates when he says that, after Shakespeare, Balzac is our most important magazine of documents on human nature. Balzac's aim, in fact, was to do for humanity what Buffon had done for the animal creation. As the naturalist studied lions and tigers, so the novelist studied men and women. Yet he was no mere reporter. Photography and *procès-verbal* were not the essentials of his method. Observation gave him the facts of life, but his genius converted facts into truths, and truths into truth. He was, in a word, a marvellous combination of the artistic temperament with the scientific spirit. The latter he bequeathed to his disciples; the former was entirely his own. The distinction between such a book as M. Zola's *L'Assommoir* and such a book as Balzac's *Illusions Perdues* is the distinction between unimaginative realism and imaginative reality. 'All Balzac's characters,' said Baudelaire, 'are gifted with the same ardour of life that animated himself. All his fictions are as deeply coloured as dreams. Every mind is a weapon loaded to the muzzle with will. The very scullions have genius.' He was, of course, accused of being immoral. Few writers who deal directly with life escape that charge. His answer to the accusation was characteristic and conclusive. 'Whoever contributes his stone to the edifice of ideas,' he wrote, 'whoever proclaims an abuse, whoever sets his mark upon an evil to be abolished, always passes for immoral. If you are true in your portraits, if, by dint of daily and nightly toil, you succeed in writing the most difficult language in the world, the word immoral is thrown in your face.' The morals of the personages of the *Comédie Humaine* are simply the morals of the world around us. They are part of the artist's subject-matter; they are not part of his method. If there be any need of censure it is to life, not to literature, that it should be given. Balzac, besides, is essentially universal. He sees life from every point of view. He has no preferences and no prejudices. He does not try to prove anything. He feels that the spectacle of life contains its own secret. 'Il crée un monde et se tait.'

And what a world it is! What a panorama of passions! What a pell-mell of men and women! It was said of Trollope that he increased the number of our acquaintances without adding to our visiting list; but after the *Comédie Humaine* one begins to believe that the only real people are the people who have never existed. Lucien de Rubempré, le Père Goriot, Ursule Mirouët, Marguerite Claës, the Baron Hulot, Madame Marneffe, le Cousin Pons, De Marsay – all bring with them a kind of contagious illusion of life. They have a fierce vitality about them: their existence is fervent and fiery-coloured; we not merely feel for them but we see them – they dominate our fancy and defy scepticism. A steady course of Balzac reduces our living friends to shadows, and our acquaintances to the shadows of shades. Who would care to go out to an evening party to meet Tomkins, the friend of one's boyhood, when one can sit at home with Lucien de Rubempré? It is pleasanter to have the entrée to Balzac's society than to receive cards from all the duchesses in Mayfair.

In spite of this, there are many people who have declared the *Comédie Humaine* to be indigestible. Perhaps it is: but then what about truffles? Balzac's publisher refused to be disturbed by any such criticism as that. 'Indigestible, is it?' he exclaimed with what, for a publisher, was rare good sense. 'Well, I should hope so; who ever thinks of a dinner that isn't?' And our English publisher, Mr Routledge, clearly agrees with M. Poulet-Malassis, as he is occupied in producing a complete translation of the

Comédie Humaine. The two volumes that at present lie before us contain *César Birotteau*, that terrible tragedy of finance, and *L'Illustre Gaudissart*, the apotheosis of the commercial traveller, the *Duchesse de Langeais*, most marvellous of modern love stories, *Le Chef d'Œuvre Inconnu*, from which Mr Henry James took his *Madonna of the Future*, and that extraordinary romance *Une Passion dans le Désert*. The choice of stories is quite excellent, but the translations are very unequal, and some of them are positively bad. *L'Illustre Gaudissart*, for instance, is full of the most grotesque mistakes, mistakes that would disgrace a schoolboy. 'Bon conseil vaut un œil dans le main' is translated 'Good advice is an egg in the hand'! 'Écus rebelles' is rendered 'rebellious lucre', and such common expressions as 'faire la barbe', 'attendre la ventre', 'n'entrendre rien', 'pâlir sur une affaire', are all mistranslated. 'Des bois de quoi se faire un cure-dent' is not 'a few trees to slice into toothpicks', but 'as much timber as would make a toothpick'; 'son horloge enfermée dans une grande armoire oblongue' is not 'a clock which he kept shut up in a large oblong closet' but simply a clock in a tall clock-case; 'journal viager' is not 'an annuity', 'garce' is not the same as 'farce', and 'dessins des Indes' are not 'drawings of the Indies'. On the whole, nothing can be worse than this translation, and if Mr Routledge wishes the public to read his version of the *Comédie Humaine*, he should engage translators who have some slight knowledge of French.

César Birotteau is better, though it is not by any means free from mistakes. 'To suffer under the Maximum' is an absurd rendering of 'subir le maximum'; 'perse' is 'chintz', not 'Persian chintz'; 'rendre le pain bénit' is not 'to take the wafer'; 'rivière' is hardly a '*fillet* of diamonds'; and to translate 'son cœur avait un calus à l'endroit du loyer' by 'his heart was a callus in the direction of a lease' is an insult to two languages. On the whole, the best version is that of the *Duchesse de Langeais*, though even this leaves much to be desired. Such a sentence as 'to imitate the rough logician who marched before the Pyrrhonians *while denying his own movement*' entirely misses the point of Balzac's 'imiter le rude logicien qui marchait devant les pyrrhoniens, qui niaient le mouvement.'

We fear Mr Routledge's edition will not do. It is well printed

and nicely bound; but his translators do not understand French.
It is a great pity, for *La Comédie Humaine* is one of the masterpieces
of the age.

Balzac's Novels in English. *The Duchesse de Langeais and Other Stories;
César Birotteau*. (Routledge and Sons.)

From the Poets' Corner

Pall Mall Gazette, 30 May 1887, 20 January, 15 February 1888

A cynical critic once remarked that no great poet is intelligible and no little poet worth understanding, but that otherwise poetry is an admirable thing. This, however, seems to us a somewhat harsh view of the subject. Little poets are an extremely interesting study. The best of them have often some new beauty to show us, and though the worst of them may bore yet they rarely brutalize. *Poor Folks' Lives*, for instance, by the Rev. Frederick Langbridge, is a volume that could do no possible harm to any one. These poems display a healthy, rollicking, G. R. Sims tone of feeling, an almost unbounded regard for the converted drunkard, and a strong sympathy with the sufferings of the poor. As for their theology, it is of that honest, downright and popular kind, which in these rationalistic days is probably quite as useful as any other form of theological thought. Here is the opening of a poem called *A Street Sermon*, which is an interesting example of what muscular Christianity can do in the sphere of verse-making:

What, God fight shy of the city?
  He's t'other side up I guess;
If you ever want to find Him,
  Whitechapel's the right address.

Those who prefer pseudo-poetical prose to really prosaic poetry will wish that Mr Dalziel had converted most of his *Pictures in the Fire* into leaders for the *Daily Telegraph*, as, from the literary point of view, they have all the qualities dear to the Asiatic school. What a splendid leader the young lions of Fleet Street would have made out of *The Prestige of England*, for instance, a poem suggested by the opening of the Zulu war in 1879.

Now away sail our ships far away o'er the sea,
   Far away with our gallant and brave;
The loud war-cry is sounding like wild revelriè,
   And our heroes dash on to their grave;
For the fierce Zulu tribes have arisen in their might,
   And in thousands swept down on our few;
But these braves only yielded when crushed in the fight,
   Man to man to their colours were true.

The conception of the war-cry sounding 'like wild revelriè' is quite in the true Asiatic spirit, and indeed the whole poem is full of the daring English of a special correspondent. Personally, we prefer Mr Dalziel when he is not quite so military. *The Fairies*, for instance, is a very pretty poem, and reminds us of some of Dicky Doyle's charming drawings, and *Nat Bentley* is a capital ballad in its way. The Irish poems, however, are rather vulgar and should be expunged. The Celtic element in literature is extremely valuable, but there is absolutely no excuse for shrieking 'Shillelagh!' and 'O Gorrah!'

Women must Weep, by Professor Harald Williams, has the most dreadful cover of any book that we have come across for some time past. It is possibly intended to symbolize the sorrow of the world, but it merely suggests the decorative tendencies of an undertaker and is as depressing as it is detestable. However, as the cowl does not make the monk, so the binding, in the case of the Savile Club school, does not make the poet, and we open the volume without prejudice. The first poem that we come to is a vigorous attack on those wicked and misguided people who believe that Beauty is its own reason for existing, and that Art should have no other aim but her own perfection. Here are some of the Professor's gravest accusations:

Why do they patch, in their fatal choice,
   When at secrets such the angels quake,
But a play of the Vision and the Voice? –
   Oh, it's all for Art's sake.

Why do they gather what should be left,
   And leave behind what they ought to take,
And exult in the basest blank or theft? –
   Oh, it's all for Art's sake.

It certainly must be admitted that to 'patch' or to 'exult in the basest blank' is a form of conduct quite unbefitting an artist, the very obscurity and incomprehensible character of such a crime adding something to its horror. However, while fully recognizing the wickedness of 'patching' we cannot but think that Professor Harald Williams is happier in his criticism of life than he is in his art criticism. His poem *Between the Banks*, for instance, has a touch of sincerity and fine feeling that almost atones for its overemphasis.

Mr Buchan's blank verse drama *Joseph and His Brethren* bears no resemblance to that strange play on the same subject which Mr Swinburne so much admires. Indeed, it may be said to possess all the fatal originality of inexperience. However, Mr Buchan does not leave us in any doubt about his particular method of writing. 'As to the dialogue,' he says, 'I have put the language of real life into the mouths of the speakers, except when they may be supposed to be under strong emotion; then their utterances become more rapid – broken – figurative – in short more poetical.' Well, here is the speech of Potiphar's wife under strong emotion:

ZULEEKHA (*seizing him*). Love me! or death!
Ha! dost thou think thou wilt not, and yet live?
By Isis, no. And thou wilt turn away,
Iron, marble mockman! Ah! I hold thy life!
Love feeds on death. It swallows up all life,
Hugging, or killing. I to woo, and thou –
Unhappy me! Oh!

The language here is certainly rapid and broken, and the expression 'marble mockman' is, we suppose, figurative, but the passage can scarcely be described as poetical, though it fulfils all Mr Buchan's conditions. Still, tedious as Zuleekha and Joseph are, the Chorus of Ancients is much worse. These 'ideal spectators' seem to spend their lives in uttering those solemn platitudes that with the aged pass for wisdom. The chief offenders are the members of what Mr Buchan calls 'The 2nd – Semi-chorus,' who have absolutely no hesitation in interrupting the progress of the play with observations of this kind:

2ND – SEMI-CHORUS
Ah! but favour extreme shown to one
  Among equals who yet stand apart,
    Awakeneth, say ye, if naturally,
      The demons – jealousy, envy, hate, –
  In the breast of those passed by.

It is a curious thing that when minor poets write choruses to a play they should always consider it necessary to adopt the style and language of a bad translator. We fear that Mr Bohn has much to answer for.

God's Garden is a well-meaning attempt to use Nature for theological and educational purposes. It belongs to that antiquated school of thought that, in spite of the discoveries of modern science, invites the sluggard to look at the ant, and the idle to imitate the bee. It is full of false analogies and dull eighteenth-century didactics. It tells us that the flowering cactus should remind us that a dwarf may possess mental and moral qualities, that the mountain ash should teach us the precious fruits of affliction, and that a fond father should learn from the example of the chestnut that the most beautiful children often turn out badly! We must admit that we have no sympathy with this point of view, and we strongly protest against the idea that

The flaming poppy, with its black core, tells
Of anger's flushing face, and heart of sin.

The worst use that man can make of Nature is to turn her into a mirror for his own vices, nor are Nature's secrets ever disclosed to those who approach her in this spirit. However, the author of this irritating little volume is not always botanizing and moralizing in this reckless and improper fashion. He has better moments, and those who sympathize with the Duke of Westminster's efforts to provide open spaces for the people, will no doubt join in the aspiration

God bless wise Grosvenors whose hearts incline,
Workmen to fête, and grateful souls refine;

though they may regret that so noble a sentiment is expressed in so inadequate a form.

It is difficult to understand why Mr Cyrus Thornton should have called his volume *Voices of the Street*. However, poets have a perfect right to christen their own children, and if the wine is good no one should quarrel with the bush. Mr Thornton's verse is often graceful and melodious, and some of his lines, such as

And the wise old Roman bondsman saw no terror in the dead –
Children when the play was over, going softly home to bed,

have a pleasant Tennysonian ring. The *Ballad of the Old Year* is rather depressing. 'Bury the Old Year Solemnly' has been said far too often, and the sentiment is suitable only for Christmas crackers. The best thing in the book is *The Poet's Vision of Death*, which is quite above the average.

Mrs Dobell informs us that she has already published sixteen volumes of poetry and that she intends to publish two more. The volume that now lies before us is entitled *In the Watches of the Night*, most of the poems that it contains having been composed 'in the neighbourhood of the sea, between the hours of ten and two o'clock.' Judging from the following extract we cannot say that we consider this is a very favourable time for inspiration, at any rate in the case of Mrs Dobell:

Were Anthony Trollope and George Eliot
Alive – which unfortunately they are not –
As regards the subject of 'quack-snubbing,' you know,
To support me I am sure they hadn't been slow –
For they, too, hated the wretched parasite
That fattens on the freshest, the most bright
Of the blossoms springing from the – Public Press! –
And that oft are flowers that even our quacks should bless!

Mr Evans's *Caesar Borgia* is a very tedious tragedy. Some of the passages are in the true 'Ercles' vein', like the following:

CAESAR (*starting up*).
    Help, Michelotto, help! Begone! Begone!
    Friends! torments! devils! Gandia! What, Gandia?
    O turn those staring eyes away. See! See
    He bleeds to death! O fly! Who are those fiends
    That tug me by the throat? O! O! O! O! (*Pauses.*)

But, as a rule, the style is of a more commonplace character. The other poems in the volume are comparatively harmless, though it is sad to find Shakespeare's 'Bacchus with pink eyne' reappearing as 'pinky-eyed Silenus.'

The Cross and the Grail is a collection of poems on the subject of temperance. Compared to real poetry these verses are as 'water unto wine', but no doubt this was the effect intended. The illustrations are quite dreadful, especially one of an angel appearing to a young man from Chicago who seems to be drinking brown sherry.

Juvenal in Piccadilly and *The Excellent Mystery* are two fierce social satires and, like most satires, they are the product of the corruption they pillory. The first is written on a very convenient principle. Blank spaces are left for the names of the victims and these the reader can fill up as he wishes.

> Must — — bluster, — — give the lie,
> — — wear the night out, — — sneer!

is an example of this anonymous method. It does not seem to us very effective. *The Excellent Mystery* is much better. It is full of clever epigrammatic lines, and its wit fully atones for its bitterness. It is hardly a poem to quote but it is certainly a poem to read.

The Chronicle of Mites is a mock-heroic poem about the inhabitants of a decaying cheese who speculate about the origin of their species and hold learned discussions upon the meaning of evolution and the Gospel according to Darwin. This cheese-epic is a rather unsavoury production and the style is at times so monstrous and so realistic that the author should be called the Gorgon-Zola of literature.

Such a pseudonym for a poet as 'Glenessa' reminds us of the good old days of the Della Cruscans, but it would not be fair to attribute Glenessa's poetry to any known school of literature, either past or present. Whatever qualities it possesses are entirely its own. Glenessa's most ambitious work, and the one that gives the title to his book, is a poetic drama about the Garden of Eden. The subject is undoubtedly interesting, but the execution can

hardly be said to be quite worthy of it. Devils, on account of
their inherent wickedness, may be excused for singing

Then we'll rally – rally – rally –
Yes, we'll rally – rally O! –

but such scenes as

Enter ADAM

ADAM (*excitedly*) Eve, where art thou?
EVE (*surprised*) Oh!
ADAM (*in astonishment*) Eve! my God, she's there
  Beside that fatal tree;

or

Enter ADAM *and* EVE

EVE (*in astonishment*) Well, is not this surprising?
ADAM (*distracted*) It is –

seem to belong rather to the sphere of comedy than to that of
serious verse. Poor Glenessa! the gods have not made him poetical, and we hope he will abandon his wooing of the muse. He is
fitted, not for better, but for other things.

Mr Brodie's *Lyrics of the Sea* are spirited and manly, and show
a certain freedom of rhythmical movement, pleasant in days of
wooden verse. He is at his best, however, in his sonnets. Their
architecture is not always of the finest order but, here and there,
one meets with lines that are graceful and felicitous.

Like silver swallows on a summer morn
Cutting the air with momentary wings,

is pretty, and on flowers Mr Brodie writes quite charmingly. The
only thoroughly bad piece in the book is *The Workman's Song.*
Nothing can be said in favour of

Is there a bit of blue, boys?
  Is there a bit of blue?
In heaven's leaden hue, boys?
  'Tis hope's eye peeping through . . .

for optimism of this kind is far more dispiriting than Schopenhauer or Hartmann at his worst, nor are there really any grounds for supposing that the British workman enjoys third-rate poetry.

Poor Folks' Lives. By the Rev. Frederick Langbridge. (Simpkin, Marshall and Co.)

Pictures in the Fire. By George Dalziel. (Privately Printed.)

Women Must Weep. By Profesor F. Harald Williams. (Swan Sonnenschein and Co.)

Joseph and His Brethren: a Trilogy. By Alexander Buchan. (Digby and Long.)

God's Garden. By Heartsease. (James Nisbet and Co.)

Voices of the Street. By Cyrus Thornton. (Elliot Stock.)

In the Watches of the Night. By Mrs Horace Dobell. (Remington and Co.)

Caesar Borgia. By W. Evans, MA. (William Maxwell and Son.)

The Cross and the Grail. (Women's Temperance Association, Chicago.)

Juvenal in Piccadilly. By Oxoniensis. (Vizetelly and Co.)

The Excellent Mystery: A Matrimonial Satire. By Lord Pimlico. (Vizetelly and Co.)

The Chronicle of Mites. By James Aitchison. (Kegan Paul.)

The Discovery and Other Poems. By Glenessa. (National Publishing Co.)

Lyrics of the Sea. By E. H. Brodie. (Bell and Sons.)

Sir Edwin Arnold's
Last Volume

Pall Mall Gazette, 11 December 1888

Writers of poetical prose are rarely good poets. They may crowd their page with gorgeous epithet and resplendent phrase, may pile Pelions of adjectives upon Ossas of descriptions, may abandon themselves to highly coloured diction and rich luxuriance of imagery, but if their verse lacks the true rhythmical life of verse, if their method is devoid of the self-restraint of the real artist, all their efforts are of very little avail. 'Asiatic' prose is possibly useful for journalistic purposes, but 'Asiatic' poetry is not to be encouraged. Indeed, poetry may be said to need far more self-restraint than prose. Its conditions are more exquisite. It produces its effects by more subtle means. It must not be allowed to degenerate into mere rhetoric or mere eloquence. It is, in one sense, the most self-conscious of all the arts, as it is never a means to an end but always an end in itself. Sir Edwin Arnold has a very picturesque or, perhaps we should say, a very pictorial style. He knows India better than any living Englishman knows it, and Hindustani better than any English writer should know it. If his descriptions lack distinction, they have at least the merit of being true, and when he does not interlard his pages with an interminable and intolerable series of foreign words he is pleasant enough. But he is not a poet. He is simply a poetical writer – that is all.

However, poetical writers have their uses, and there is a good deal in Sir Edwin Arnold's last volume that will repay perusal. The scene of the story is placed in a mosque attached to the monument of the Taj Mahal, and a group composed of a learned Mirza, two singing girls with their attendant, and an Englishman, is supposed to pass the night there reading the chapter of Sa'di upon 'Love', and conversing upon that theme with

accompaniments of music and dancing. The Englishman is, of
course, Sir Edwin Arnold himself:

> lover of India,
> Too much her lover! for his heart lived there
> How far soever wandered thence his feet.

Lady Dufferin appears as

> Lady Duffreen, the mighty Queen's Vice-queen!

which is really one of the most dreadful blank-verse lines that
we have come across for some time past. M. Renan is 'a priest
of Frangestan,' who writes in 'glittering French'; Lord Tennyson
is

> One we honour for his songs –
> Greater than Sa'di's self –

and the Darwinians appear as the 'Mollahs of the West,' who

> hold Adam's sons
> Sprung of the sea-slug.

All this is excellent fooling in its way, a kind of play-acting in
literature; but the best parts of the book are the descriptions of
the Taj itself, which are extremely elaborate, and the various
translations from Sa'di with which the volume is interspersed.
The great monument Shah Jahan built for Arjamand is

> Instinct with loveliness – not masonry!
> Not architecture! as all others are,
> But the proud passion of an Emperor's love
> Wrought into living stone, which gleams and soars
> With body of beauty shrining soul and thought,
> Insomuch that it haps as when some face
> Divinely fair unveils before our eyes –
> Some woman beautiful unspeakably –
> And the blood quickens, and the spirit leaps,
> And will to worship bends the half-yielded knees,
> Which breath forgets to breathe; so is the Taj;
> You see it with the heart, before the eyes
> Have scope to gaze. All white! snow white! cloud white!

We cannot say much in praise of the sixth line:

Insomuch that it haps as when some face:

it is curiously awkward and unmusical. But this passage from Sa'di is remarkable:

When Earth, bewildered, shook in earthquake-throes,
With mountain-roots He bound her borders close;
  Turkis and ruby in her rocks He stored,
And on her green branch hung His crimson rose.

He shapes dull seed to fair imaginings;
Who paints with moisture as He painteth things?
  Look! from the cloud He sheds one drop on ocean,
As from the Father's loins one drop He brings; –

And out of that He forms a peerless pearl,
And, out of this, a cypress boy or girl;
  Utterly wotting all their innermosts,
For all to Him is visible! Uncurl

Your cold coils, Snakes! Creep forth, ye thrifty Ants!
Handless and strengthless He provides your wants
  Who from the 'Is not' planned the 'Is to be,'
And Life is non-existent void implants.

Sir Edwin Arnold suffers, of course, from the inevitable comparison that one cannot help making between his work and the work of Edward Fitzgerald, and certainly Fitzgerald could never have written such a line as 'utterly wotting all their innermosts', but it is interesting to read almost any translation of those wonderful Oriental poets with their strange blending of philosophy and sensuousness, of simple parable or fable and obscure mystic utterance. What we regret most in Sir Edwin Arnold's book is his habit of writing in what really amounts to a sort of 'pigeon English'. When we are told that 'Lady Duffreen, the mighty Queen's Vice-queen,' paces among the *charpoys* of the ward 'no whit afraid of *sitla*, or of *tap*'; when the Mirza explains

  âg lejao!
To light the kallians for the Saheb and me,

and the attendant obeys with '*Achcha! Achcha!*' when we are invited to listen to 'the *Vina* and the drum' and told about *ekkas*,

Byrâgis, hamals and *Tamboora,* all that we can say is that to such *ghazals* we are not prepared to say either *Shamash* or *Afrîn.* In English poetry we do not want

> *chatkis* for the toes,
> *Jasams* for elbow-bands, and *gote* and *har,*
> *Bala* and *mala.*

This is not local colour; it is a sort of local discoloration. It does not add anything to the vividness of the scene. It does not bring the Orient more clearly before us. It is simply an inconvenience to the reader and a mistake on the part of the writer. It may be difficult for a poet to find English synonyms for Asiatic expressions, but even if it were impossible it is none the less a poet's duty to find them. We are sorry that a scholar and a man of culture like Sir Edwin Arnold should have been guilty of what is really an act of treason against our literature. But for this error, his book, though not in any sense a work of genius or even of high artistic merit, would still have been of some enduring value. As it is, Sir Edwin Arnold has translated Sa'di and someone must translate Sir Edwin Arnold.

With Sa'di in the Garden; or The Book of Love. By Sir Edwin Arnold, MA, KCIE, author of *The Light of Asia, etc.* (Trübner and Co.)

Half-Hours with the
Worst Authors

Pall Mall Gazette, 15 January 1886

I am very much pleased to see that you are beginning to call attention to the extremely slipshod and careless style of our ordinary magazine-writers. Will you allow me to refer your readers to an article on Borrow, in the current number of *Macmillan*, which exemplifies very clearly the truth of your remarks? The author of the article is Mr George Saintsbury, a gentleman who has recently written a book on Prose Style, and here are some specimens of the prose of the future according to the *système Saintsbury*:

1. He saw the rise, and, *in some instances, the death, of Tennyson*, Thackeray, Macaulay, Carlyle, Dickens.
2. *See* a *place* which Kingsley, *or* Mr Ruskin, *or* some other master of our decorative school, *have* described – *much more* one which has fallen into the hands of the small fry of their imitators – and you are almost sure to find that *it has been overdone*.
3. The great mass of his translations, published and unpublished, and the smaller mass of his early hackwork, no doubt *deserves* judicious excerption.
4. 'The Romany Rye' *did not appear* for six years, *that is to say, in* 1857.
5. The elaborate apparatus which most prose tellers of fantastic tales *use*, and generally *fail in using*.
6. The great writers, whether they try to be like other people or try not to be like them (*and sometimes in the first case most of all*), succeed *only* in being themselves.
7. If he had a slight *overdose* of Celtic blood and Celtic peculiarity, it was *more than made up* by the readiness of literary expression which it gave him. He, if any one, bore an English heart, though, *as there often has been*, there was something perhaps more than English as well as less than it in his fashion of expression.

8. His flashes of ethical reflection, which, though like *all* ethical reflections *often* one-sided.

9. He certainly was an *unfriend* to Whiggery.

10. *That it contains* a great deal of quaint and piquant writing *is only to say* that its writer wrote it.

11. 'Wild Wales', too, because of *its* easy and direct *opportunity* of comparing its description with the originals.

12. The capital *and* full-length portraits.

13. Whose attraction is *one* neither mainly nor in any very great degree one of pure form.

14. *Constantly* right *in general*.

These are merely a few examples of the style of Mr Saintsbury, a writer who seems quite ignorant of the commonest laws both of grammar and of literary expression, who has apparently no idea of the difference between the pronouns 'this' and 'that', and has as little hesitation in ending the clause of a sentence with a preposition, as he has in inserting a parenthesis between a preposition and its object, a mistake of which the most ordinary schoolboy would be ashamed. And why can not our magazine-writers use plain, simple English? *Unfriend*, quoted above, is a quite unnecessary archaism, and so is such a phrase as *With this Borrow could not away*, in the sense of 'this Borrow could not endure'. 'Borrow's *abstraction* from general society' may, I suppose, pass muster. Pope talks somewhere of a hermit's 'abstraction', but what is the meaning of saying that the author of Lavengro *quartered* Castile and Leon 'in the most interesting manner, riding everywhere with his servant'? And what defence can be made for such an expression as 'Scott, and other *black beasts* of Borrow's'? Black beast for *bête noire* is really abominable.

The object of my letter, however, is not to point out the deficiencies of Mr Saintsbury's style, but to express my surprise that his article should have been admitted into the pages of a magazine like *Macmillan's*. Surely it does not require much experience to know that such an article is a disgrace even to magazine literature.

George Borrow. By George Saintsbury. (*Macmillan's Magazine*, January 1886.)

A lecture delivered in America during Wilde's tour in 1882. It was announced as a lecture on 'The Practical Application of the Principles of the Aesthetic Theory to Exterior and Interior House Decoration, With Observations upon Dress and Personal Ornaments.' The earliest date on which it is known to have been given is 11 May 1882.

House Decoration

In my last lecture I gave you something of the history of Art in England. I sought to trace the influence of the French Revolution upon its development. I said something of the song of Keats and the school of the pre-Raphaelites. But I do not want to shelter the movement, which I have called the English Renaissance, under any palladium however noble, or any name however revered. The roots of it have, indeed, to be sought for in things that have long passed away, and not, as some suppose, in the fancy of a few young men – although I am not altogether sure that there is anything much better than the fancy of a few young men.

When I appeared before you on a previous occasion, I had seen nothing of American art save the Doric columns and Corinthian chimney-pots visible on your Broadway and Fifth Avenue. Since then, I have been through your country to some fifty or sixty different cities, I think. I find that what your people need is not so much high imaginative art but that which hallows the vessels of everyday use. I suppose that the poet will sing and the artist will paint regardless whether the world praises or blames. He has his own world and is independent of his fellow men. But the handicraftsman is dependent on your pleasure and opinion. He needs your encouragement and he must have beautiful surroundings. Your people love art but do not sufficiently honour the handicraftsman. Of course, those millionaires who can pillage Europe for their pleasure need have no care to encourage such; but I speak for those whose desire for beautiful things is larger than their means. I find that one great trouble all over is that your workmen are not given to noble designs. You cannot be indifferent to this, because Art is not something which you can take or leave. It is a necessity of human life.

And what is the meaning of this beautiful decoration which we call art? In the first place, it means value to the workman and it means the pleasure which he must necessarily take in making a beautiful thing. The mark of all good art is not that the thing done is done exactly or finely, for machinery may do as much, but that it is worked out with the head and the workman's heart. I cannot impress the point too frequently that beautiful and rational designs are necessary in all work. I did not imagine, until I went into some of your simpler cities, that there was so much bad work done. I found, where I went, bad wallpapers horribly designed, and coloured carpets, and that old offender the horsehair sofa, whose stolid look of indifference is always so depressing. I found meaningless chandeliers and machine-made furniture, generally of rosewood, which creaked dismally under the weight of the ubiquitous interviewer. I came across the small iron stove which they always persist in decorating with machine-made ornaments, and which is as great a bore as a wet day or any other particularly dreadful institution. When unusual extravagance was indulged in, it was garnished with two funeral urns.

It must always be remembered that what is well and carefully made by an honest workman, after a rational design, increases in beauty and value as the years go on. The old furniture brought over by the Pilgrims, two hundred years ago, which I saw in New England, is just as good and as beautiful today as it was when it first came here. Now, what you must do is to bring artists and handicraftsmen together. Handicraftsmen cannot live, certainly cannot thrive, without such companionship. Separate these two and you rob art of all spiritual motive.

Having done this, you must place your workman in the midst of beautiful surroundings. The artist is not dependent on the visible and the tangible. He has his visions and his dreams to feed on. But the workman must see lovely forms as he goes to his work in the morning and returns at eventide. And, in connection with this, I want to assure you that noble and beautiful designs are never the result of idle fancy or purposeless daydreaming. They come only as the accumulation of habits of long and delightful observation. And yet such things may not be taught. Right ideas concerning them can certainly be obtained only by those who have been accustomed to rooms that are beautiful and colours that are satisfying.

Perhaps one of the most difficult things for us to do is to choose a notable and joyous dress for men. There would be more joy in life if we were to accustom ourselves to use all the beautiful colours we can in fashioning our own clothes. The dress of the future, I think, will use drapery to a great extent and will abound with joyous colour. At present we have lost all nobility of dress and, in doing so, have almost annihilated the modern sculptor. And, in looking around at the figures which adorn our parks, one could almost wish that we had completely killed the noble art. To see the frockcoat of the drawing-room done in bronze, or the double waistcoat perpetuated in marble, adds a new horror to death. But indeed, in looking through the history of costume, seeking an answer to the questions we have propounded, there is little that is either beautiful or appropriate. One of the earliest forms is the Greek drapery which is so exquisite for young girls. And then, I think we may be pardoned a little enthusiasm over the dress of the time of Charles I, so beautiful indeed, that in spite of its invention being with the Cavaliers it was copied by the Puritans. And the dress for the children of that time must not be passed over. It was a very golden age of the little ones. I do not think that they have ever looked so lovely as they do in the pictures of that time. The dress of the last century in England is also peculiarly gracious and graceful. There is nothing bizarre or strange about it, but it is full of harmony and beauty. In these days, when we have suffered so dreadfully from the incursions of the modern milliner, we hear ladies boast that they do not wear a dress more than once. In the old days, when the dresses were decorated with beautiful designs and worked with exquisite embroidery, ladies rather took a pride in bringing out the garment and wearing it many times and handing it down to their daughters – a process that would, I think, be quite appreciated by a modern husband when called upon to settle his wife's bills.

And how shall men dress? Men say that they do not particularly care how they dress, and that it is little matter. I am bound to reply that I do not think that you do. In all my journeys through the country, the only well-dressed men that I saw – and in saying this I earnestly deprecate the polished indignation of your Fifth Avenue dandies – were the Western miners. Their wide-brimmed hats, which shaded their faces from the sun and protected them from the rain, and the cloak, which is by far the most beautiful piece of drapery ever invented, may well be dwelt on with admiration. Their high boots, too, were sensible and practical. They wore only what was comfortable, and therefore beautiful. As I looked at them I could not help thinking with regret of the time when these picturesque miners would have made their fortunes and would go East to assume again all the abominations of modern fashionable attire. Indeed, so concerned was I that I made some of them promise that when they again appeared in the more crowded scenes of Eastern civilization they would still continue to wear their lovely costume. But I do not believe they will.

Now, what America wants to-day is a school of rational art. Bad art is a great deal worse than no art at all. You must show your workmen specimens of good work so that they come to know what is simple and true and beautiful. To that end I would have you have a museum attached to these schools – not one of those dreadful modern institutions where there is a stuffed and very dusty giraffe, and a case or two of fossils, but a place where there are gathered examples of art decoration from various periods and countries. Such a place is the South Kensington Museum in London whereon we build greater hopes for the future than on any other one thing. There I go every Saturday night, when the museum is open later than usual, to see the handicraftsman, the woodworker, the glassblower and the worker in metals. And it is here that the man of refinement and culture comes face to face with the workman who ministers to his joy. He comes to know more of the nobility of the workman, and the workman, feeling the appreciation, comes to know more of the nobility of his work.

You have too many white walls. More colour is wanted. You should have such men as Whistler among you to teach you the beauty and joy of colour. Take Mr Whistler's 'Symphony in White', which you no doubt have imagined to be something quite bizarre. It is nothing of the sort. Think of a cool grey sky flecked here and there with white clouds, a grey ocean and three wonderfully beautiful figures robed in white, leaning over the water and dropping white flowers from their fingers. Here is no extensive intellectual scheme to trouble you, and no metaphysics of which we have had quite enough in art. But if the simple and unaided colour strike the right keynote, the whole conception is made clear. I regard Mr Whistler's famous Peacock Room as the finest thing in colour and art decoration which the world has known since Correggio painted that wonderful room in Italy where the little children are dancing on the walls. Mr Whistler finished another room just before I came away – a breakfast room in blue and yellow. The ceiling was a light blue, the cabinet-work and the furniture were of a yellow wood, the curtains at the windows were white and worked in yellow, and when the table was set for breakfast with dainty blue china nothing can be conceived at once so simple and so joyous.

The fault which I have observed in most of your rooms is that there is apparent no definite scheme of colour. Everything is not attuned to a keynote as it should be. The apartments are crowded with pretty things which have no relation to one another. Again, your artists must decorate what is more simply useful. In your art schools I found no attempt to decorate such things as the vessels for water. I know of nothing uglier than the ordinary jug or pitcher. A museum could be filled with the different kinds of water vessels which are used in hot countries. Yet we continue to submit to the depressing jug with the handle all on one side. I do not see the wisdom of decorating dinner-plates with sunsets and soup-plates with moonlight scenes. I do not think it adds anything to the pleasure of the canvas-back duck to take it out of such glories. Besides, we do not want a soup-plate whose bottom seems to vanish in the distance. One feels neither safe nor comfortable under such conditions. In fact, I did not find in the art schools of the country that the difference was explained between decorative and imaginative art.

The conditions of art should be simple. A great deal more depends upon the heart than upon the head. Appreciation of art is not secured by any elaborate scheme of learning. Art requires a good healthy atmosphere. The motives for art are still around about us as they were round about the ancients. And the subjects are also easily found by the earnest sculptor and the painter. Nothing is more picturesque and graceful than a man at work. The artist who goes to the children's playground, watches them at their sport and sees the boy stop to tie his shoe, will find the same themes that engaged the attention of the ancient Greeks, and such observation and the illustrations which follow will do much to correct that foolish impression that mental and physical beauty are always divorced.

To you, more than perhaps to any other country, has Nature been generous in furnishing material for art workers to work in. You have marble quarries where the stone is more beautiful in colour than any the Greeks ever had for their beautiful work, and yet day after day I am confronted with the great building of some stupid man who has used the beautiful material as if it were not precious almost beyond speech. Marble should not be used save by noble workmen. There is nothing which gave me a greater sense of barrenness in travelling through the country than the entire absence of wood carving on your houses. Wood carving is the simplest of the decorative arts. In Switzerland the little barefooted boy beautifies the porch of his father's house with examples of skill in this direction. Why should not American boys do a great deal more and better than Swiss boys?

There is nothing to my mind more coarse in conception and more vulgar in execution than modern jewellery. This is something that can easily be corrected. Something better should be made out of the beautiful gold which is stored up in your mountain hollows and strewn along your river beds. When I was at Leadville and reflected that all the shining silver that I saw coming from the mines would be made into ugly dollars, it made me sad. It should be made into something more permanent. The golden gates at Florence are as beautiful to-day as when Michelangelo saw them.

We should see more of the workman than we do. We should not be content to have the salesman stand between us – the salesman who knows nothing of what he is selling save that he is charging a great deal too much for it. And watching the workman will teach that most important lesson – the nobility of all rational workmanship.

I said in my last lecture that art would create a new brotherhood among men by furnishing a universal language. I said that under its beneficent influences war might pass away. Thinking this, what place can I ascribe to art in our education? If children grow up among all fair and lovely things, they will grow to love beauty and detest ugliness before they know the reason why. If you go into a house where everything is coarse, you find things chipped and broken and unsightly. Nobody exercises any care. If everything is dainty and delicate, gentleness and refinement of manner are unconsciously acquired. When I was in San Francisco I used to visit the Chinese Quarter frequently. There I used to watch a great hulking Chinese workman at his task of digging, and used to see him every day drink his tea from a little cup as delicate in texture as the petal of a flower, whereas in all the grand hotels of the land, where thousands of dollars have been lavished on great gilt mirrors and gaudy columns, I have been given my coffee or my chocolate in cups an inch and a quarter thick. I think I have deserved something nicer.

The art systems of the past have been devised by philosophers who looked upon human beings as obstructions. They have tried to educate boys' minds before they had any. How much better it would be in these early years to teach children to use their hands in the rational service of mankind. I would have a workshop attached to every school, and one hour a day given up to the teaching of simple decorative arts. It would be a golden hour to the children. And you would soon raise up a race of handicraftsmen who would transform the face of your country. I have seen only one such school in the United States, and this was in Philadelphia and was founded by my friend Mr Leyland. I stopped there yesterday and have brought some of the work here this afternoon to show you. Here are two discs of beaten brass: the designs on them are beautiful, the workmanship is simple, and the entire result is satisfactory. The work was done by a little boy twelve years old. This is a wooden bowl decorated by a little girl of thirteen. The design is lovely and the colouring delicate and pretty. Here you see a piece of beautiful wood carving accomplished by a little boy of nine. In such work as this, children learn sincerity in art. They learn to abhor the liar in art – the man who paints wood to look like iron, or iron to look like stone. It is a practical school of morals. No better way is there to learn to love Nature than to understand Art. It dignifies every flower of the field. And, the boy who sees the thing of beauty which a bird on the wing becomes when transferred to wood or canvas will probably not throw the customary stone. What we want is something spiritual added to life. Nothing is so ignoble that Art cannot sanctify it.

A Handbook to Marriage

Pall Mall Gazette, 18 November 1885

In spite of its somewhat alarming title this book may be highly recommended to everyone. As for the authorities the author quotes, they are almost numberless, and range from Socrates down to Artemus Ward. He tells us of the wicked bachelor who spoke of marriage as 'a very harmless amusement' and advised a young friend of his to 'marry early and marry often'; of Dr Johnson who proposed that marriage should be arranged by the Lord Chancellor, without the parties concerned having any choice in the matter; of the Sussex labourer who asked, 'Why should I give a woman half my victuals for cooking the other half?' and of Lord Verulam who thought that unmarried men did the best public work. And, indeed, marriage is the one suject on which all women agree and all men disagree. Our author, however, is clearly of the same opinion as the Scotch lassie who, on her father warning her what a solemn thing it was to get married, answered, 'I ken that, father, but it's a great deal solemner to be single.' He may be regarded as the champion of the married life. Indeed, he has a most interesting chapter on marriage-made men, and though he dissents, and we think rightly, from the view recently put forward by a lady or two on the Women's Rights platform that Solomon owed all his wisdom to the number of his wives, still he appeals to Bismarck, John Stuart Mill, Mahommed and Lord Beaconsfield, as instances of men whose success can be traced to the influence of the women they married. Archbishop Whately once defined woman as 'a creature that does not reason and pokes the fire from the top,' but since his day the higher education of women has considerably altered their position. Women have always had an emotional sympathy with those they love; Girton and Newnham have rendered intellectual sympathy also possible. In our day it is best for a man to be married, and men must give up the tyranny in married life which was once so dear to them, and which, we are afraid, lingers still, here and there.

'Do you wish to be my wife, Mabel?' said a little boy. ' Yes,' incautiously answered Mabel. 'Then pull off my boots.'

On marriage vows our author has, too, very sensible views and very amusing stories. He tells of a nervous bridegroom who, confusing the baptismal and marriage ceremonies, replied when asked if he consented to take the bride for his wife: 'I renounce them all'; of a Hampshire rustic who, when giving the ring, said solemnly to the bride: 'With my body I thee wash up, and with all my hurdle goods I thee and thou'; of another who, when asked whether he would take his partner to be his wedded wife, replied with shameful indecision: 'Yes, I'm willin'; but I'd a sight rather have her sister'; and of a Scotch lady who, on the occasion of her daughter's wedding, was asked by an old friend whether she might congratulate her on the event, and answered: 'Yes, yes, upon the whole it is very satisfactory; it is true Jeannie hates her gudeman, but then there's always a something!' Indeed, the good stories contained in this book are quite endless and make it very pleasant reading, while the good advice is on all points admirable.

Most young married people nowadays start in life with a dreadful collection of ormolu inkstands covered with sham onyxes, or with a perfect museum of salt-cellars. We strongly recommend this book as one of the best of wedding presents. It is a complete handbook to an earthly Paradise, and its author may be regarded as the Murray of matrimony and the Baedeker of bliss.

How to be Happy though Married: Being a Handbook to Marriage. By a Graduate in the University of Matrimony. (T. Fisher Unwin.)

Dinners and Dishes

Pall Mall Gazette, 7 March 1885

Aman can live for three days without bread, but no man can live for one day without poetry, was an aphorism of Baudelaire. You can live without pictures and music but you cannot live without eating, says the author of *Dinners and Dishes*; and this latter view is, no doubt, the more popular. Who, indeed, in these degenerate days would hesitate between an ode and an omelette, a sonnet and a salmi? Yet the position is not entirely Philistine; cookery is an art; are not its principles the subject of South Kensington lectures, and does not the Royal Academy give a banquet once a year? Besides, as the coming democracy will, no doubt, insist on feeding us all on penny dinners, it is well that the laws of cookery should be explained: for were the national meal burned, or badly seasoned, or served up with the wrong sauce a dreadful revolution might follow.

Under these circumstances we strongly recommend *Dinners and Dishes* to every one: it is brief and concise and makes no attempt at eloquence, which is extremely fortunate. For even on ortolans who could endure oratory? It also has the advantage of not being illustrated. The subject of a work of art has, of course, nothing to do with its beauty, but still there is always something depressing about the coloured lithograph of a leg of mutton.

As regards the author's particular views, we entirely agree with him on the important question of macaroni. 'Never,' he says, 'ask me to back a bill for a man who has given me a macaroni pudding.' Macaroni is essentially a savoury dish and may be served with cheese or tomatoes but never with sugar and milk. There is also a useful description of how to cook risotto – a delightful dish too rarely seen in England; an excellent chapter on the different kinds of salads, which should be carefully studied by those many hostesses whose imaginations never pass beyond lettuce and beetroot; and actually a recipe for making Brussels sprouts eatable. The last is, of course, a masterpiece.

The real difficulty that we all have to face in life is not so much the science of cookery as the stupidity of cooks. And in this little handbook to practical Epicureanism the tyrant of the English kitchen is shown in her proper light. Her entire ignorance of herbs, her passion for extracts and essences, her total inability to make a soup which is anything more than a combination of pepper and gravy, her inveterate habit of sending up bread poultices with pheasants – all these sins and many others are ruthlessly unmasked by the author. Ruthlessly and rightly. For the British cook is a foolish woman who should be turned for her iniquities into a pillar of salt which she never knows how to use.

But our author is not local merely. He has been in many lands; he has eaten back-hendl at Vienna and kulibatsch at St Petersburg; he has had the courage to face the buffalo veal of Roumania and to dine with a German family at one o'clock; he has serious views on the right method of cooking those famous white truffles of Turin of which Alexandre Dumas was so fond; and, in the face of the Oriental Club, declares that Bombay curry is better than the curry of Bengal. In fact he seems to have had experience of almost every kind of meal except the 'square meal' of the Americans. This he should study at once; there is a great field for the philosophic epicure in the United States. Boston beans may be dismissed at once as delusions, but soft-shell crabs, terrapin, canvas-back ducks, blue fish and the pompono of New Orleans are all wonderful delicacies, particularly when one gets them at Delmonico's. Indeed, the two most remarkable bits of scenery in the States are undoubtedly Delmonico's and the Yosemité Valley; and the former place has done more to promote a good feeling between England and America than anything else has in this century.

We hope that 'Wanderer' will go there soon and add a chapter to *Dinners and Dishes*, and that his book will have in England the influence it deserves. There are twenty ways of cooking a potato and three hundred and sixty-five ways of cooking an egg, yet the

British cook, up to the present moment, knows only three methods of sending up either one or the other.

Dinners and Dishes. By 'Wanderer'. (Simpkin and Marshall.)

L'Envoi

An Introduction to *Rose Leaf and Apple Leaf*
by Rennell Rodd, published by
J. M. Stoddart and Co., Philadelphia, 1882

Amongst the many young men in England who are seeking
along with me to continue and to perfect the English
Renaissance – *jeunes guerriers du drapeau romantique*, as Gautier
would have called us – there is none whose love of art is more
flawless and fervent, whose artistic sense of beauty is more subtle
and more delicate – none, indeed, who is dearer to myself – than
the young poet whose verses I have brought with me to America;
verses full of sweet sadness, and yet full of joy; for the most
joyous poet is not he who sows the desolate highways of this
world with the barren seed of laughter, but he who makes his
sorrow most musical, this indeed being the meaning of joy in art
– that incommunicable element of artistic delight which, in
poetry, for instance, comes from what Keats called the 'sensuous
life of verse', the element of song in the singing, made so pleasurable to us by that wonder of motion which often has its origin
in mere musical impulse, and in painting is to be sought for,
from the subject never, but from the pictorial charm only – the
scheme and symphony of the colour, the satisfying beauty of the
design: so that the ultimate expression of our artistic movement
in painting has been, not in the spiritual visions of the Pre-
Raphaelites, for all their marvel of Greek legend and their
mystery of Italian song, but in the work of such men as Whistler
and Albert Moore, who have raised design and colour to the
ideal level of poetry and music. For the quality of their exquisite
painting comes from the mere inventive and creative handling
of line and colour, from a certain form and choice of beautiful
workmanship, which, rejecting all literary reminiscence and all
metaphysical idea, is in itself entirely satisfying to the aesthetic
sense – is, as the Greeks would say, an end in itself; the effect of

their work being like the effect given to us by music; for music is the art in which form and matter are always one – the art whose subject cannot be separated from the method of its expression; the art which most completely realizes for us the artistic ideal, and is the condition to which all the other arts are constantly aspiring.

Now, this increased sense of the absolutely satisfying value of beautiful workmanship, this recognition of the primary import-ance of the sensuous element in art, this love of art for art's sake, is the point in which we of the younger school have made a departure from the teaching of Mr Ruskin – a departure definite and different and decisive.

Master indeed of the knowledge of all noble living and of the wisdom of all spiritual things will he be to us ever, seeing that it was he who by the magic of his presence and the music of his lips taught us at Oxford that enthusiasm for beauty which is the secret of Hellenism, and that desire for creation which is the secret of life, and filled some of us, at least, with the lofty and passionate ambition to go forth into far and fair lands with some message for the nations and some mission for the world, and yet in his art criticism, his estimate of the joyous element of art, his whole method of approaching art, we are no longer with him; for the keystone to his aesthetic system is ethical always. He would judge of a picture by the amount of noble moral ideas it expresses; but to us the channels by which all noble work in painting can touch, and does touch, the soul are not those of truths of life or metaphysical truths. To him perfection of work-manship seems but the symbol of pride, and incompleteness of technical resource the image of an imagination too limitless to find within the limits of form its complete expression, or of a love too simple not to stammer in its tale. But to us the rule of art is not the rule of morals. In an ethical system, indeed, of any gentle mercy good intentions will, one is fain to fancy, have their recognition; but of those that would enter the serene House of Beauty the question that we ask is not what they had ever meant to do, but what they have done. Their pathetic intentions are of no value to us, but their realized creations only. *Pour moi je préfère les poètes qui font des vers, les médecins qui sachent guérir, les peintres qui sachent peindre.*

Nor, in looking at a work of art, should we be dreaming of what it symbolizes, but rather loving it for what it is. Indeed, the transcendental spirit is alien to the spirit of art. The metaphysical mind of Asia may create for itself the monstrous and many-breasted idol, but to the Greek, pure artist, that work is most instinct with spiritual life which conforms most closely to the perfect facts of physical life also. Nor, in its primary aspect, has a painting, for instance, any more spiritual message or meaning for us than a blue tile from the wall of Damascus, or a Hitzen vase. It is a beautifully coloured surface, nothing more, and affects us by no suggestion stolen from philosophy, no pathos pilfered from literature, no feeling filched from a poet, but by its own incommunicable artistic essence – by that selection of truth which we call style, and that relation of values which is the draughtsmanship of painting, by the whole quality of the workmanship, the arabesque of the design, the splendour of the colour, for these things are enough to stir the most divine and remote of the chords which make music in our soul, and colour, indeed, is of itself a mystical presence on things, and tone a kind of sentiment.

This, then – the new departure of our younger school – is the chief characteristic of Mr Rennell Rodd's poetry; for, while there is much in his work that may interest the intellect, much that will excite the emotions, and many-cadenced chords of sweet and simple sentiment – for to those who love Art for its own sake all other things are added – yet, the effect which they pre-eminently seek to produce is purely an artistic one. Such a poem as *The Sea-King's Grave*, with all its majesty of melody as sonorous and as strong as the sea by whose pine-fringed shores it was thus nobly conceived and nobly fashioned; or the little poem that follows it, whose cunning workmanship, wrought with such an artistic sense of limitation, one might liken to the rare chasing of the mirror that is its motive; or *In a Church*, pale flower of one of those exquisite moments when all things except the moment itself seem so curiously real, and when the old memories of forgotten days are touched and made tender, and the familiar place grows fervent and solemn suddenly with a vision of the undying beauty of the gods that died; or the scene in *Chartres Cathedral*, sombre silence brooding on vault and arch, silent people kneeling on the dust of the desolate pavement as the young priest lifts Lord Christ's body in a crystal star, and then the sudden beams of scarlet light that break through the blazoned window and smite on the carven screen, and sudden organ peals of mighty music rolling and echoing from choir to canopy, and from spire to shaft, and over all the clear glad voice of a singing boy, affecting one as a thing over-sweet, and striking just the right artistic keynote for one's emotions; or *At Lanuvium*, through the music of whose lines one seems to hear again the murmur of the Mantuan bees straying down from their own green valleys and inland streams to find what honeyed amber the sea-flowers might be hiding; or the poem written *In the Coliseum*, which gives one the same artistic joy that one gets watching a handicraftsman at his work, a goldsmith hammering out his gold into those thin plates as delicate as the petals of a yellow rose, or drawing it out into the long wires like tangled sunbeams, so perfect and precious is the mere handling of it; or the little lyric interludes that break in here and there like the singing of a thrush, and are as swift and as sure as the beating of a bird's wing, as light and bright as the apple blossoms that flutter fitfully down to the orchard grass after a spring shower, and look the lovelier for the rain's tears lying on their dainty veinings of pink and pearl; or the sonnets – for Mr Rodd is one of those *qui sonnent le sonnet*, as the Ronsardists used to say – that one called *On the Border Hills*, with its fiery wonder of imagination and the strange beauty of its eighth line; or the one which tells of the sorrow of the great king for the little dead child – well, all these poems aim, as I said, at producing a purely artistic effect, and have the rare and exquisite quality that belongs to work of that kind; and I feel that the entire subordination in our aesthetic movement of all merely emotional and intellectual motives to the vital informing poetic principle is the surest sign of our strength.

But it is not enough that a work of art should conform to the aesthetic demands of the age: there should be also about it, if it is to give us any permanent delight, the impress of a distinct individuality. Whatever work we have in the nineteenth century must rest on the two poles of personality and perfection. And so in this little volume, by separating the earlier and more simple work from the work that is later and stronger and possesses increased technical power and more artistic vision, one might weave these disconnected poems, these stray and scattered threads, into one fiery-coloured strand of life, noting first a boy's mere gladness of being young, with all its simple joy in field and flower, in sunlight and in song, and then the bitterness of sudden sorrow at the ending by Death of one of the brief and beautiful friendships of one's youth, with all those unanswered longings and questionings unsatisfied by which we vex, so uselessly, the marble face of death; the artistic contrast between the discontented incompleteness of the spirit and the complete perfection of the style that expresses it forming the chief element of the aesthetic charm of these particular poems; – and then the birth of Love, and all the wonder and the fear and the perilous delight of one on whose boyish brows the little wings of love have beaten for the first time; and the love-songs, so dainty and delicate, little swallow-flights of music, and full of such fragrance and freedom that they might all be sung in the open air and across moving water; and then autumn, coming with its choirless woods and odorous decay and ruined loveliness, Love lying dead; and the sense of the mere pity of it.

One might stop there, for from a young poet one should ask for no deeper chords of life than those that love and friendship make eternal for us; and the best poems in the volume belong clearly to a later time, a time when these real experiences become absorbed and gathered up into a form which seems from such real experiences to be the most alien and the most remote; when the simple expression of joy or sorrow suffices no longer, and lives rather in the stateliness of the cadenced metre, in the music and colour of the linked words, than in any direct utterance; lives, one might say, in the perfection of the form more than in the pathos of the feeling. And yet, after the broken music of love and the burial of love in the autumn woods, we can trace that wandering among strange people, and in lands unknown to us, by which we try so pathetically to heal the hurts of the life we

know, and that pure and passionate devotion to Art which one
gets when the harsh reality of life has too suddenly wounded
one, and is with discontent or sorrow marring one's youth, just
as often, I think, as one gets it from any natural joy of living;
and that curious intensity of vision by which, in moments of
overmastering sadness and despair ungovernable, artistic things
will live in one's memory with a vivid realism caught from the
life which they help one to forget – an old grey tomb in Flanders
with a strange legend on it, making one think how, perhaps,
passion does live on after death; a necklace of blue and amber
beads and a broken mirror found in a girl's grave at Rome, a
marble image of a boy habited like Eros, and with the pathetic
tradition of a great king's sorrow lingering about it like a purple
shadow, – over all these the tired spirit broods with that calm
and certain joy that one gets when one has found something that
the ages never dull and the world cannot harm; and with it
comes that desire of Greek things which is often an artistic
method of expressing one's desire for perfection; and that longing
for the old dead days which is so modern, so incomplete, so
touching, being, in a way, the inverted torch of Hope, which
burns the hand it should guide; and for many things a little
sadness, and for all things a great love; and lastly, in the pine-
wood by the sea, once more the quick and vital pulse of joyous
youth leaping and laughing in every line, the frank and fearless
freedom of wave and wind waking into fire life's burnt-out ashes
and into song the silent lips of pain – how clearly one seems to
see it all, the long colonnade of pines with sea and sky peeping
in here and there like a flitting of silver; the open place in the
green, deep heart of the wood with the little moss-grown altar
to the old Italian god in it; and the flowers all about, cyclamen
in the shadowy places, and the stars of the white narcissus lying
like snowflakes over the grass, where the quick, bright-eyed lizard
starts by the stone, and the snake lies coiled lazily in the sun on
the hot sand, and overhead the gossamer floats from the branches
like thin, tremulous threads of gold – the scene is so perfect for
its motive, for surely here, if anywhere, the real gladness of life
might be revealed to one's youth – the gladness that comes, not
from the rejection, but from the absorption, of all passion, and

is like that serene calm that dwells in the faces of the Greek statues, and which despair and sorrow cannot touch, but intensify only.

In some such way as this we could gather up these strewn and scattered petals of song into one perfect rose of life, and yet, perhaps, in so doing, we might be missing the true quality of the poems; one's real life is so often the life that one does not lead; and beautiful poems, like threads of beautiful silks, may be woven into many patterns and to suit many designs, all wonderful and all different: and romantic poetry, too, is essentially the poetry of impressions, being like that latest school of painting, the school of Whistler and Albert Moore, in its choice of situation as opposed to subject; in its dealing with the exceptions rather than with the types of life; in its brief intensity; in what one might call its fiery-coloured momentariness, it being indeed the momentary situations of life, the momentary aspects of nature, which poetry and painting now seek to render for us. Sincerity and constancy will the artist, indeed, have always; but sincerity in art is merely that plastic perfection of execution without which a poem or a painting, however noble its sentiment or human its origin, is but wasted and unreal work, and the constancy of the artist cannot be to any definite rule or system of living, but to that principle of beauty only through which the inconstant shadows of his life are in their most fleeting moment arrested and made permanent.

He will not, for instance, in intellectual matters acquiesce in that facile orthodoxy of our day which is so reasonable and so artistically uninteresting, nor yet will he desire that fiery faith of the antique time which, while it intensified, yet limited the vision; still less will he allow the calm of his culture to be marred by the discordant despair of doubt or the sadness of a sterile scepticism; for the Valley Perilous, where ignorant armies clash by night, is no resting-place meet for her to whom the gods have assigned the clear upland, the serene height, and the sunlit air – rather will he be always curiously testing new forms of belief, tinging his nature with the sentiment that still lingers about some beautiful creeds, and searching for experience itself, and not for the fruits of experience; when he has got its secret, he will leave without regret much that was once very precious to him. 'I am always insincere,' says Emerson somewhere, 'as knowing that there are other moods': '*Les émotions*,' wrote Théophile Gautier once in a review of Arsène Houssaye, '*Les émotions ne se ressemblent pas, mais être ému – voilà l'important.*'

Now, this is the secret of the art of the modern romantic school, and gives one the right keynote for its apprehension; but the real quality of all work which, like Mr Rodd's, aims, as I said, at a purely artistic effect, cannot be described in terms of intellectual criticism; it is too intangible for that. One can perhaps convey it best in terms of the other arts, and by reference to them; and, indeed, some of these poems are as iridescent and as exquisite as a lovely fragment of Venetian glass; others as delicate in perfect workmanship and as single in natural motive as an etching by Whistler is, or one of those beautiful little Greek figures which in the olive woods round Tanagra men can still find, with the faint gilding and the fading crimson not yet fled from hair and lips and raiment; and many of them seem like one of Corot's twilights just passing into music; for not merely in visible colour, but in sentiment also – which is the colour of poetry – may there be a kind of tone.

But I think that the best likeness to the quality of this young poet's work I ever saw was in the landscape by the Loire. We were staying once, he and I, at Amboise, that little village with its grey slate roofs and steep streets and gaunt, grim gateway, where the quiet cottages nestle like white pigeons into the sombre clefts of the great bastioned rock, and the stately Renaissance houses stand silent and apart – very desolate now, but with some memory of the old days still lingering about the delicately twisted pillars, and the carved doorways, with their grotesque animals, and laughing masks, and quaint heraldic devices, all reminding one of a people who could not think life real till they had made it fantastic. And above the village, and beyond the bend of the river, we used to go in the afternoon, and sketch from one of the big barges that bring the wine in autumn and the wood in winter down to the sea, or lie in the long grass and make plans *pour la gloire, et pour ennuyer les philistins*, or wander along the low, sedgy banks, 'matching our reeds in sportive rivalry', as comrades used in the old Sicilian days; and the land was an ordinary land enough, and bare, too, when one thought of Italy, and how the oleanders were robing the hillsides by Genoa in scarlet, and the cyclamen filling with its purple every valley from Florence to Rome; for there was not much real beauty, perhaps, in it, only long, white dusty roads and straight rows of formal poplars; but, now and then, some little breaking gleam of broken light would lend to the grey field and the silent barn a secret and a mystery that were hardly their own, would transfigure for one exquisite moment the peasants passing down through the vineyard, or the shepherd watching on the hill, would tip the willows with silver and touch the river into gold; and the wonder of the effect, with the strange simplicity of the material, always seemed to me to be a little like the quality of these the verses of my friend.

Index